Artificial Intelligence in Corporate Communications

Redefining the Game

Book 6 in the AI Series

Bonnie Kurowski

Artificial Intelligence in Corporate Communication

A Note from the Author

Dear Reader,

I understand that the rise of artificial intelligence has sparked concerns about its potential impact on various aspects of our professional lives, particularly in the realm of company communications. It's only natural to feel a sense of uncertainty and apprehension as we navigate through this era of technological transformation. I want to assure you that you are not alone in these concerns. Many individuals across different industries share similar worries about how AI might affect their jobs and the dynamics of workplace communication.

The fear of job displacement and the unknown can be overwhelming, but it's essential to recognize that we are at the forefront of an evolution rather than an outright upheaval. In this book, I aim to provide you with insights, perspectives, and practical strategies to navigate the changing landscape of company communications in the age of AI.

Artificial Intelligence in Corporate Communication

Rather than viewing artificial intelligence as a threat, let's explore how it can be a powerful tool to enhance our capabilities, streamline processes, and open up new opportunities for growth and innovation. By gaining a deeper understanding of AI and its potential applications, you will be better equipped to adapt and thrive in a world where technology complements our skills and augments our capabilities. This book serves as a guide to help alleviate your fears by providing a roadmap for harnessing the positive aspects of AI within the context of company communications.

Remember, you are not alone in this journey.
Together, we can embrace the future with confidence, knowing that by leveraging AI intelligently, we can enhance our professional lives rather than fearing its impact.
Sincerely,

Bonnie Kurowski, Author

Redefining the Game

Artificial Intelligence in Corporate Communication

AI Book Series

Book 1: Navigating the Future: AI's Influence on Adult Learning and Instructional Design Careers

Book 2: AI-Enhanced Instructional Design: A Guide for the Modern ADDIE Professional

Book 3: AI-Driven Learning & Development: Navigating ADDIE, SAM, Agile, and SAFe using the H.E.A.D.S. Framework

Book 4: Driving Transformation: Leveraging AI in Change Management

Book 5: AI-Powered Project Management: Revolutionizing Agile Methodologies

Book 6: Artificial Intelligence in Corporate Communications: Redefining the Game

Table Of Contents

A Note from the Author	1
AI Book Series	3
Chapter 1: Introduction to Artificial Intelligence in Corporate Communication	7
Chapter 2: Understanding Artificial Intelligence	24

Chapter 3: The AI Revolution in Corporate Communication Strategies	40
Chapter 4: AI-powered Communication Tools and Technologies	60
Chapter 5: Leveraging AI for Internal Communication	78
Chapter 6: AI-driven External Communication Strategies	94
Chapter 7: The Future of Artificial Intelligence in Corporate Communication	115
Chapter 8: Best Practices for Implementing AI in Corporate Communication	130

Chapter 9: Case Studies: Successful AI Integration in Corporate Communication   151

Chapter 10: Conclusion   166

Chapter 1: Introduction to Artificial Intelligence in Corporate Communication

The Growing Importance of Artificial Intelligence in Corporate Communication

In this rapidly evolving digital landscape, the role of artificial intelligence (AI) in corporate communication has become increasingly important. With advancements in technology, businesses are starting to realize the immense potential AI holds in redefining their communication strategies. From streamlining internal processes to enhancing customer experiences, AI is revolutionizing the way corporations communicate.

One of the key benefits of AI in corporate communication is its ability to automate routine tasks, freeing up valuable time and resources. AI-powered chatbots are being widely adopted by businesses to handle customer queries, providing instant and personalized responses 24/7. This not only improves customer satisfaction but also reduces the workload on human employees, allowing them to focus on more complex and strategic tasks.

Artificial Intelligence in Corporate Communication

Moreover, AI-driven analytics are empowering corporations to gain actionable insights from vast amounts of data. By leveraging machine learning algorithms, businesses can analyze customer preferences, market trends, and competitor behavior, enabling them to make data-driven decisions. This data-driven approach not only enhances the effectiveness of corporate communication but also leads to improved business outcomes.

AI is also transforming internal communication within organizations. Virtual assistants and voice recognition tools are becoming commonplace, facilitating seamless communication and collaboration among employees. These technologies allow for efficient scheduling, document sharing, and task management, enabling teams to work together more effectively, regardless of their physical location.

Furthermore, AI is enabling corporations to personalize their communication efforts at scale. By analyzing customer data, AI algorithms can generate personalized content and recommendations, ensuring that each interaction with the customer feels tailored to their specific needs and preferences. This personalized approach strengthens customer relationships, drives engagement, and ultimately improves business outcomes.

However, while AI offers tremendous potential, corporations must also be mindful of the ethical implications associated with its use. Transparency, privacy, and security concerns need to be addressed to ensure that AI is used responsibly and ethically in corporate communication.

Artificial Intelligence in Corporate Communication

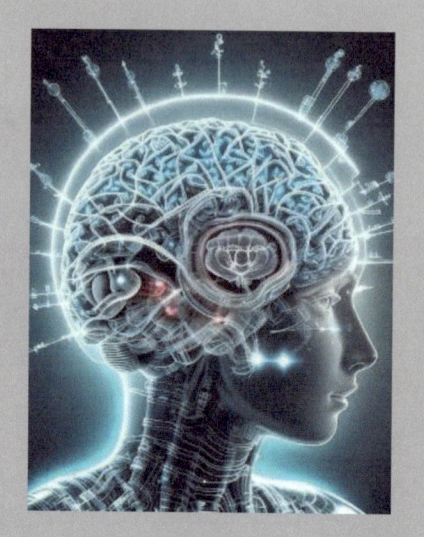

As the AI revolution continues to unfold, it is clear that the growing importance of AI in corporate communication strategies cannot be ignored. Embracing AI technologies allows corporations to streamline processes, enhance customer experiences, and make data-driven decisions. By leveraging the power of AI, corporations can redefine the game of corporate communication, enabling them to stay ahead in this increasingly competitive and digital world.

Redefining the Game

Artificial Intelligence in Corporate Communication

Objectives of the Book

The subchapter "Objectives of the Book" in "Artificial Intelligence in Corporate Communication: Redefining the Game" sets out to present a comprehensive overview of the objectives and goals that this book aims to achieve. Targeted at corporate professionals and leaders who are eager to understand and harness the power of artificial intelligence (AI) in their communication strategies, this subchapter serves as a roadmap for what readers can expect to gain from the book.

Artificial Intelligence in Corporate Communication

1. Understanding the AI Revolution in Corporate Communication Strategies:

The primary objective of this book is to provide the corporate audience with a deep understanding of the AI revolution and how it is reshaping corporate communication strategies. It explores the fundamental concepts of AI and its impact on various aspects of corporate communication, including internal and external communication, customer engagement, reputation management, and crisis communication.

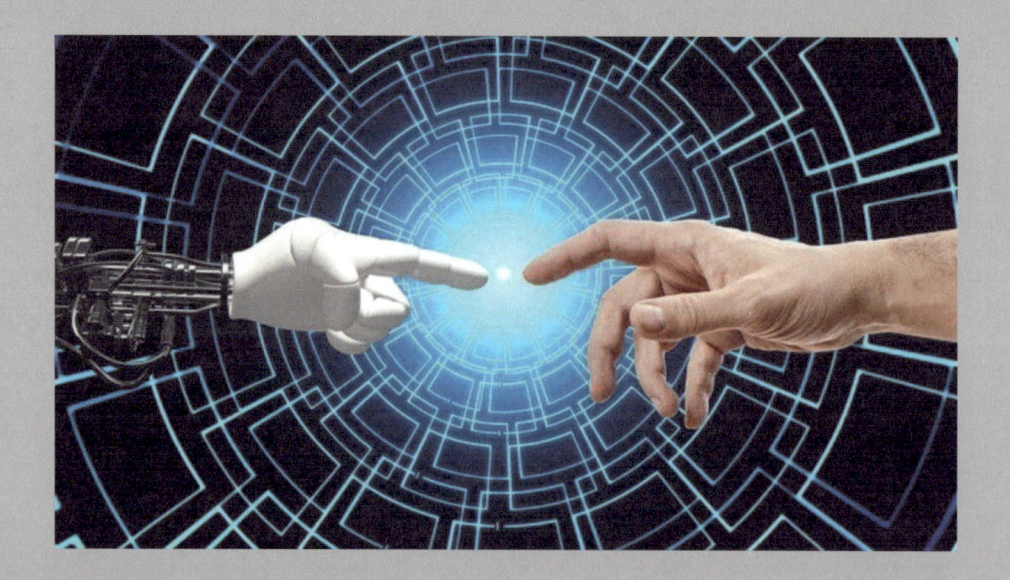

2. Identifying Opportunities for AI Integration:

Another key objective is to help corporate professionals identify opportunities for integrating AI into their communication strategies. Through real-world case studies and examples, the book highlights how AI technologies such as natural language processing, machine learning, chatbots, and sentiment analysis can be effectively utilized to improve communication efficiency, personalization, and overall organizational performance.

Artificial Intelligence in Corporate Communication

3. Overcoming Challenges and Ethical Considerations:

The book aims to address the challenges and ethical considerations associated with AI implementation in corporate communication. It provides insights into potential risks, such as privacy concerns, data security, and the fear of job displacement. By discussing these issues in-depth, the book equips readers with the knowledge and tools required to navigate these challenges and ensure responsible AI adoption.

4. Practical Implementation Strategies:

To bridge the gap between theory and practice, the book focuses on providing practical implementation strategies for incorporating AI into corporate communication initiatives. It offers step-by-step guidance on how to evaluate AI solutions, select the right technology partners, and effectively integrate AI into existing communication frameworks. These strategies are designed to help corporate professionals optimize their communication efforts and stay ahead in the rapidly evolving business landscape.

5. Future Trends and Innovations:

Lastly, the book aims to inspire readers by discussing future trends and innovations in AI-driven corporate communication. By exploring cutting-edge technologies, emerging practices, and visionary ideas, it encourages corporate professionals to think beyond the present and envision the possibilities that lie ahead. This objective empowers readers to proactively adapt to upcoming changes and proactively leverage AI to gain a competitive edge.

Artificial Intelligence in Corporate Communication

In conclusion, the subchapter "Objectives of the Book" in "Artificial Intelligence in Corporate Communication: Redefining the Game" outlines the key goals of the book. By delving into the AI revolution in corporate communication strategies, identifying opportunities, addressing challenges, providing practical implementation strategies, and discussing future trends, this book aims to equip corporate professionals with the necessary knowledge and insights to navigate the evolving landscape of AI and redefine their communication game.

Overview of the Chapters

In this book, "Artificial Intelligence in Corporate Communication: Redefining the Game," we delve into the exciting realm of how artificial intelligence (AI) is revolutionizing corporate communication strategies. In an era where businesses are constantly seeking innovative ways to engage with their target audience, AI has emerged as a game-changer, redefining the rules of the corporate communication landscape.

Artificial Intelligence in Corporate Communication

This subchapter, "Overview of the Chapters," aims to provide corporate professionals with a brief glimpse into the comprehensive knowledge and insights that lie ahead in the subsequent chapters.

Chapter 1: The AI Revolution in Corporate Communication Strategies

We begin by laying the foundation of the AI revolution in corporate communication strategies. This chapter explores the historical context, key drivers, and the transformative potential of AI in reshaping how businesses communicate with their stakeholders. We highlight the central role AI technologies play in enhancing efficiency, personalization, and overall effectiveness in corporate communication.

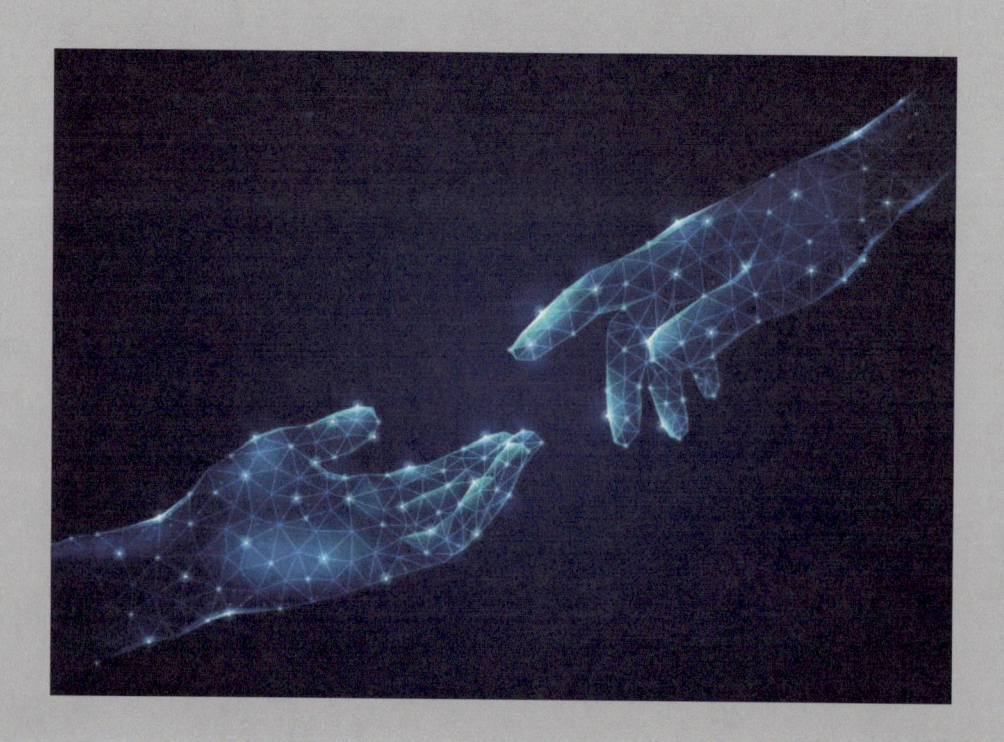

Chapter 2: Understanding AI Technologies for Corporate Communication

To harness the power of AI, it is crucial to understand the underlying technologies. This chapter delves into the various AI technologies that are disrupting corporate communication. We explore natural language processing, machine learning, chatbots, sentiment analysis, and more. By gaining a deeper understanding of these technologies, corporate professionals will be better equipped to leverage AI in their communication strategies.

Artificial Intelligence in Corporate Communication

Chapter 3: AI-powered Employee Communication and Engagement

Employee communication is integral to the success of any organization. In this chapter, we examine how AI is transforming internal communication processes. We explore how AI-driven tools and platforms can enhance employee engagement, streamline information sharing, and foster a collaborative work environment. By embracing AI in employee communication, businesses can boost productivity and strengthen their corporate culture.

Redefining the Game

Artificial Intelligence in Corporate Communication

Chapter 4: AI-driven Customer Communication and Experience

Customers are at the heart of any business, and effective communication is key to building lasting relationships. This chapter explores how AI is revolutionizing customer communication and experience. We delve into AI-powered chatbots, personalized recommendations, sentiment analysis, and other AI-driven techniques to enhance customer engagement, satisfaction, and loyalty.

Chapter 5: Ethical Considerations and Future Trends

As AI becomes more pervasive in corporate communication strategies, ethical considerations become paramount. In this final chapter, we discuss the ethical implications of AI in corporate communication and provide guidelines to ensure responsible AI usage. Additionally, we explore emerging trends and future possibilities in the field, allowing corporate professionals to stay ahead of the curve.

Artificial Intelligence in Corporate Communication

By providing an overview of each chapter, this subchapter sets the stage for an immersive exploration of how AI is reshaping corporate communication strategies. Whether you are a corporate executive, communication professional, or business owner, this book will equip you with the knowledge and insights to navigate the AI revolution and redefine the game in corporate communication.

Chapter 2: Understanding Artificial Intelligence

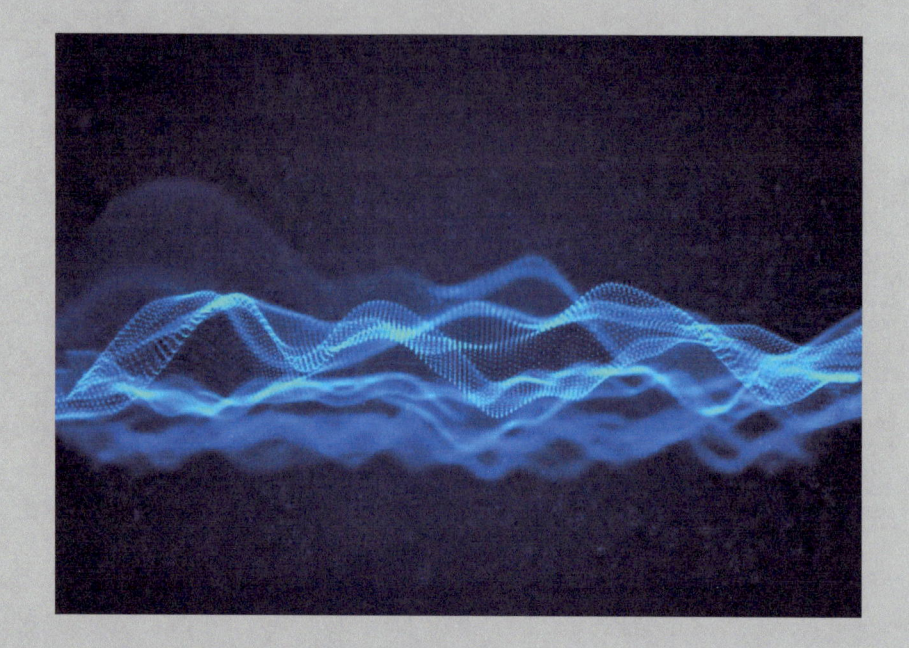

Artificial Intelligence in Corporate Communication

Definition and Evolution of Artificial Intelligence

Artificial Intelligence (AI) has emerged as a transformative force in the corporate world, revolutionizing various industries and redefining the game of corporate communication strategies. This subchapter aims to provide a comprehensive understanding of the definition and evolution of AI, shedding light on its implications for corporate communication.

Artificial Intelligence in Corporate Communication

AI can be defined as the development of intelligent machines that can perform tasks that would typically require human intelligence. These tasks include speech recognition, decision-making, problem-solving, and learning. The evolution of AI can be traced back to the 1950s when scientists began exploring the concept of creating intelligent machines. Since then, AI has experienced significant advancements, driven by breakthroughs in computing power, data availability, and algorithmic development.

Artificial Intelligence in Corporate Communication

The early stages of AI development were characterized by rule-based systems, where machines were programmed with explicit instructions to solve specific problems. However, the limitations of these systems led to the emergence of machine learning, a subset of AI that enables machines to learn from data and improve their performance over time. This shift from rule-based systems to machine learning marked a significant milestone in the evolution of AI, enabling algorithms to identify patterns, make predictions, and gain insights from vast amounts of data.

Artificial Intelligence in Corporate Communication

Another crucial development in AI is the rise of deep learning, a subset of machine learning that utilizes neural networks to simulate the human brain's structure and function. Deep learning has revolutionized AI by enabling machines to process and interpret unstructured data, such as images, videos, and natural language. This breakthrough has unlocked new possibilities for corporate communication, with applications ranging from sentiment analysis and chatbots to personalized marketing campaigns and voice assistants.

Artificial Intelligence in Corporate Communication

The evolution of AI has also witnessed the emergence of cognitive computing, which aims to replicate human thought processes, including perception, reasoning, and problem-solving. Cognitive computing systems leverage AI technologies to understand, analyze, and interpret complex data, enabling them to provide valuable insights and support decision-making processes in corporate communication strategies.

In conclusion, the definition and evolution of AI have brought about a paradigm shift in corporate communication strategies. From rule-based systems to machine learning and deep learning, AI has enabled machines to perform complex tasks, analyze vast amounts of data, and enhance decision-making processes. As the AI revolution continues to unfold, corporate communication strategies must adapt to leverage the power of AI, unlocking new opportunities for efficiency, personalization, and innovation in the corporate world.

Artificial Intelligence in Corporate Communication

Types of Artificial Intelligence

Artificial Intelligence (AI) is a rapidly evolving field that has the potential to revolutionize various aspects of corporate communication strategies. In this subchapter, we will explore the different types of AI that are driving the AI revolution in corporate communication.

1. Machine Learning: Machine learning is a branch of AI that focuses on developing algorithms that enable machines to learn from data and make predictions or decisions without being explicitly programmed. This type of AI is particularly useful in analyzing large volumes of data to identify patterns, trends, and insights that can inform corporate communication strategies.

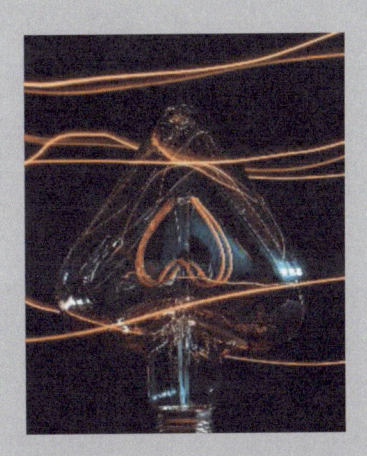

Artificial Intelligence in Corporate Communication

2. Natural Language Processing (NLP):
NLP is a subfield of AI that focuses on enabling machines to understand, interpret, and generate human language. It involves tasks such as speech recognition, language translation, sentiment analysis, and text generation. NLP is revolutionizing corporate communication by enabling chatbots and virtual assistants to understand and respond to customer queries, improving customer service and engagement.

3. Computer Vision:
Computer vision is an area of AI that focuses on enabling machines to understand and interpret visual information from images or videos. This technology is transforming corporate communication by enabling facial recognition, object detection, and image analysis.

Artificial Intelligence in Corporate Communication

For example, computer vision can be used to analyze customer behavior in retail stores or monitor employee performance in manufacturing plants.

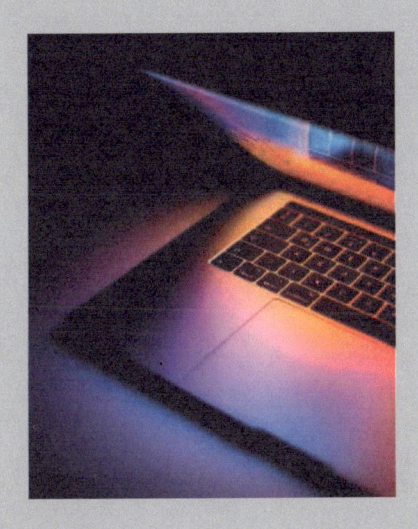

4. Expert Systems:
Expert systems are AI programs that mimic the decision-making capabilities of human experts in specific domains. They use knowledge and rules to solve complex problems and provide recommendations. In corporate communication, expert systems can be used to automate customer support processes, provide personalized recommendations, and optimize marketing campaigns.

Artificial Intelligence in Corporate Communication

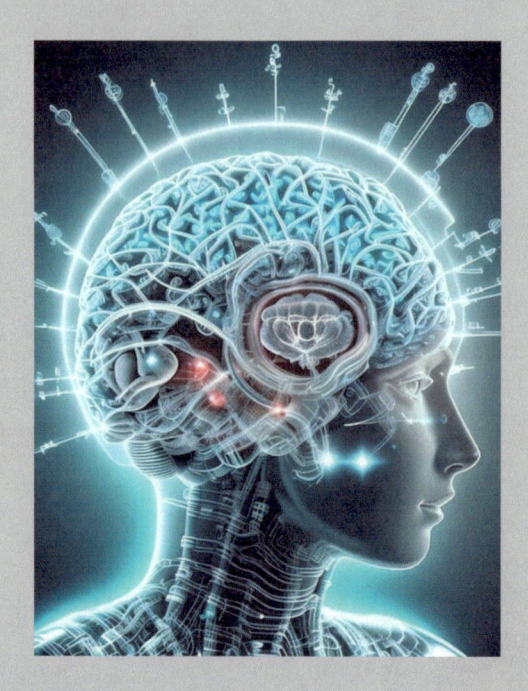

5. Neural Networks: Neural networks are AI models inspired by the structure and function of the human brain. They consist of interconnected nodes or "neurons" that process and transmit information. Neural networks are particularly effective in tasks such as image recognition, speech recognition, and natural language processing. In corporate communication, neural networks can be used to analyze customer feedback, detect sentiment, and personalize marketing messages.

Artificial Intelligence in Corporate Communication

6. Robotics Process Automation (RPA): RPA involves the use of software robots or "bots" to automate repetitive and rule-based tasks. These bots can perform tasks such as data entry, report generation, and email automation. RPA is increasingly being used in corporate communication to streamline workflows, improve efficiency, and reduce human error.

These are just a few examples of the types of AI that are revolutionizing corporate communication strategies. As AI continues to advance, it is essential for corporate professionals to understand and harness the power of these technologies to stay competitive in the ever-changing business landscape.

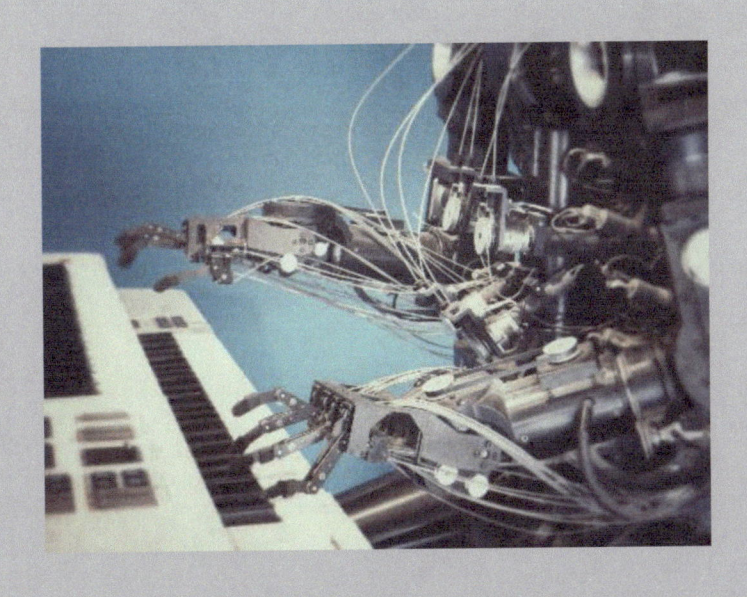

Artificial Intelligence in Corporate Communication

Applications of Artificial Intelligence in Various Industries

Artificial Intelligence (AI) has revolutionized numerous industries, transforming the way businesses operate and communicate. In this subchapter, we will explore the incredible applications of AI in various industries and how it is redefining the game in corporate communication strategies.

Artificial Intelligence in Corporate Communication

1. Healthcare Industry: AI is making significant strides in healthcare, from personalized patient care to drug discovery. AI-powered chatbots can provide immediate assistance to patients, reducing wait times and improving overall efficiency. Machine learning algorithms can also analyze medical data to identify patterns and predict diseases, enabling early diagnosis and effective treatment.

Artificial Intelligence in Corporate Communication

2. Finance and Banking: AI has greatly impacted the finance industry by automating tedious tasks, reducing human error, and enhancing security. With AI algorithms, financial institutions can detect fraudulent activities, assess creditworthiness, and provide personalized investment recommendations. AI-powered virtual assistants are also being used to handle customer queries and streamline banking processes.

3. Retail and E-commerce: AI has transformed the retail and e-commerce landscape, providing personalized shopping experiences and improving customer service. With AI-powered recommendation systems, businesses can analyze customer preferences and offer tailored product suggestions. Chatbots automate customer support, providing instant responses and resolving queries efficiently.

4. Manufacturing and Supply Chain: AI is optimizing manufacturing processes by implementing predictive maintenance and quality control systems. Machine learning algorithms analyze data from sensors to predict potential equipment failures, enabling proactive maintenance. Additionally, AI algorithms optimize supply chain management by predicting demand and optimizing inventory levels, reducing costs and improving overall efficiency.

5. Marketing and Advertising: AI-driven marketing tools are reshaping the way businesses target and engage customers. AI algorithms analyze vast amounts of customer data to deliver personalized marketing campaigns and content. Natural Language Processing (NLP) technology allows businesses to analyze customer sentiment and understand their needs better. Chatbots and virtual assistants are also being utilized for customer interactions and lead generation.

Artificial Intelligence in Corporate Communication

The AI revolution in corporate communication strategies is undeniable. From streamlining processes to enhancing customer experiences, AI is enabling businesses to operate more efficiently and effectively. Embracing AI technologies allows companies to gain a competitive edge and stay ahead in today's fast-paced business environment.

As corporate professionals, understanding the applications of AI in various industries is crucial. It allows businesses to identify opportunities for implementing AI technologies and adapt their communication strategies accordingly. By leveraging AI, companies can automate routine tasks, analyze data more effectively, and provide better customer experiences, ultimately leading to increased productivity and profitability.

In conclusion, AI is transforming industries across the board, revolutionizing corporate communication strategies in the process. By harnessing the power of AI, businesses can unlock new possibilities, drive innovation, and stay at the forefront of their respective industries.

Redefining the Game

Chapter 3: The AI Revolution in Corporate Communication Strategies

Artificial Intelligence in Corporate Communication

The Role of Artificial Intelligence in Enhancing Corporate Communication

In recent years, the corporate world has witnessed a significant revolution in communication strategies, largely driven by the advancements in artificial intelligence (AI) technology. AI, with its ability to analyze vast amounts of data, learn from patterns, and make intelligent decisions, has become a game-changer in enhancing corporate communication. This subchapter explores the profound impact of AI on corporate communication and how it is redefining the game for businesses across various industries.

Artificial Intelligence in Corporate Communication

One of the key areas where AI has transformed corporate communication is in customer service. AI-powered chatbots and virtual assistants have revolutionized the way companies interact with their customers. These intelligent systems are capable of understanding and responding to customer queries in real-time, providing personalized assistance, and even resolving complex issues. By automating routine customer interactions, AI frees up human resources to focus on more strategic and value-added tasks, improving overall efficiency and customer satisfaction.

Artificial Intelligence in Corporate Communication

Moreover, AI has enabled companies to gain valuable insights into customer preferences and behavior through advanced analytics. By analyzing vast amounts of customer data, AI algorithms can identify patterns, predict trends, and make data-driven recommendations. This allows companies to tailor their communication strategies to individual customer needs, offering personalized experiences and targeted messaging. Consequently, businesses can build stronger relationships with customers, enhance brand loyalty, and drive revenue growth.

Beyond customer service, AI has also transformed internal communication within organizations. Intelligent virtual assistants can streamline internal workflows, facilitate collaboration, and improve knowledge sharing. By leveraging natural language processing and machine learning, these assistants can help employees access relevant information, schedule meetings, and perform routine administrative tasks. This not only enhances productivity but also fosters a more cohesive and connected work environment.

Artificial Intelligence in Corporate Communication

Additionally, AI has revolutionized crisis communication for corporations. AI-powered systems can monitor and analyze vast amounts of data from various sources, including social media, news outlets, and online forums. By detecting early warning signs and analyzing sentiment, AI can provide real-time insights into emerging issues, allowing companies to proactively manage crises and mitigate reputational damage.

In conclusion, the role of artificial intelligence in enhancing corporate communication cannot be overstated. From customer service to internal communication and crisis management, AI has redefined the game for businesses across industries. By leveraging the power of AI, companies can improve efficiency, enhance customer experiences, and gain a competitive edge in today's fast-paced and digitally-driven business landscape. Embracing AI in corporate communication strategies is no longer an option but a necessity for organizations seeking to thrive in the AI revolution.

Artificial Intelligence in Corporate Communication

Benefits of Implementing AI in Corporate Communication

In today's rapidly evolving business landscape, the integration of artificial intelligence (AI) has become crucial for companies looking to stay ahead of the game. The AI revolution in corporate communication strategies has opened up new possibilities and opportunities, enabling organizations to redefine the way they communicate both internally and externally.

Redefining the Game

Artificial Intelligence in Corporate Communication

This subchapter aims to explore the benefits of implementing AI in corporate communication and how it can revolutionize the way companies operate.
One of the key advantages of incorporating AI into corporate communication is the ability to streamline and automate processes. AI-powered chatbots, for example, can handle routine customer inquiries, freeing up human resources to focus on more complex tasks. This not only enhances efficiency but also leads to significant cost savings for businesses. By automating repetitive tasks, companies can allocate their workforce to more strategic initiatives, ultimately improving productivity and driving growth.

Artificial Intelligence in Corporate Communication

Another major benefit of AI in corporate communication is the ability to personalize interactions and deliver tailored messages to target audiences. AI algorithms can analyze vast amounts of data, including customer preferences, behaviors, and demographics, to create personalized communication strategies. By providing individualized content, companies can enhance customer engagement, build stronger relationships, and increase brand loyalty.

Furthermore, AI can play a pivotal role in sentiment analysis and reputation management. By analyzing social media feeds, news articles, and other online platforms, AI algorithms can gauge public sentiment towards a company or brand. This proactive approach allows organizations to address potential issues promptly, manage crises effectively, and maintain a positive brand image.

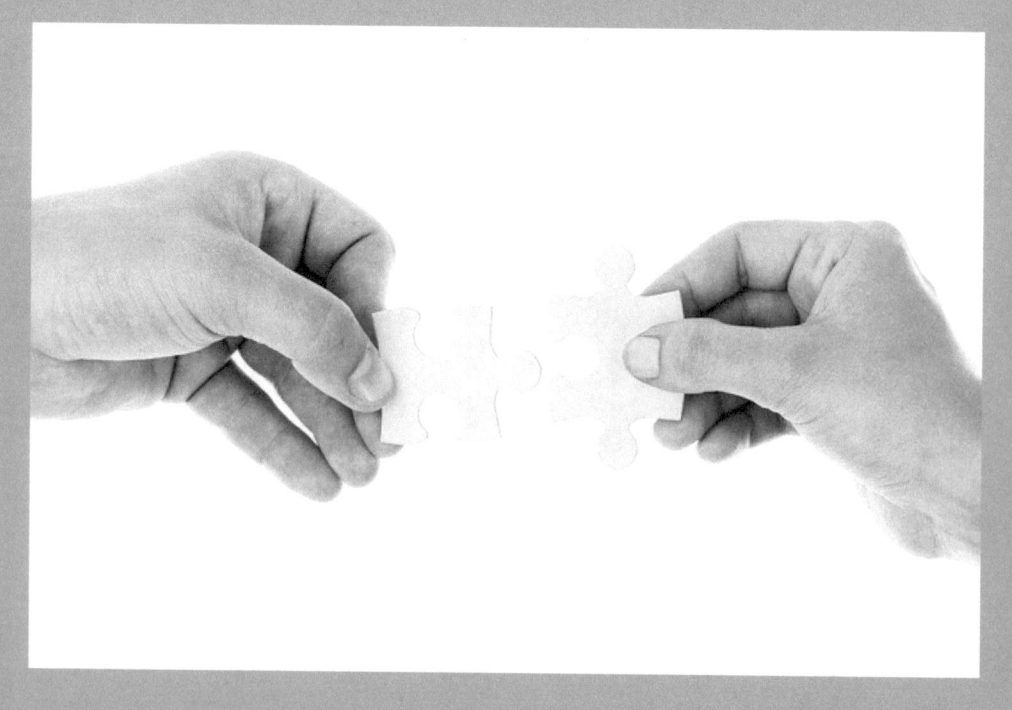

Artificial Intelligence in Corporate Communication

Additionally, AI can assist in improving internal communication within organizations. Intelligent virtual assistants can be deployed to facilitate seamless communication and collaboration among team members, regardless of geographical location. This fosters a more inclusive and efficient work environment, enabling employees to share information, exchange ideas, and collaborate on projects in real-time.

Lastly, the implementation of AI in corporate communication can provide valuable insights and analytics for strategic decision-making. AI algorithms can process and analyze large volumes of data, identifying patterns, trends, and correlations that humans may miss. These insights can help companies make data-driven decisions, optimize their communication strategies, and gain a competitive edge in the market.

Artificial Intelligence in Corporate Communication

In conclusion, the benefits of implementing AI in corporate communication are vast and transformative. From automating routine tasks and personalizing interactions to managing reputation and improving internal communication, AI is revolutionizing the way companies operate and communicate. Embracing this AI revolution in corporate communication strategies is no longer an option but a necessity for organizations looking to redefine the game and stay ahead in today's fast-paced business world.

Challenges and Risks Associated with AI in Corporate Communication

In today's rapidly evolving business landscape, incorporating artificial intelligence (AI) into corporate communication strategies has become imperative. AI technology offers a wide range of opportunities for enhancing efficiency, streamlining processes, and improving customer experiences.

However, it is essential to acknowledge the challenges and risks associated with implementing AI in corporate communication to ensure its successful integration and maximize its benefits.

Artificial Intelligence in Corporate Communication

One of the significant challenges faced when adopting AI in corporate communication is the potential for data privacy and security breaches. As AI systems rely on vast amounts of data to make informed decisions, organizations must prioritize securing sensitive information and ensuring compliance with data protection regulations. This requires implementing robust cybersecurity measures, constantly monitoring for vulnerabilities, and training employees on data protection best practices.

Redefining the Game

Artificial Intelligence in Corporate Communication

Another challenge lies in the potential for bias and discrimination within AI algorithms. AI systems are only as unbiased as the data they are trained on, and if that data contains inherent biases, it can perpetuate discrimination. Organizations must be vigilant in monitoring and mitigating bias in AI algorithms to ensure fair and ethical decision-making processes.

Artificial Intelligence in Corporate Communication

Furthermore, the rapid advancement of AI technology poses a challenge in terms of keeping up with the latest developments and trends. Corporate communication professionals need to invest in continuous learning and development to stay updated on AI capabilities and leverage them effectively. Failure to do so may result in missed opportunities or the implementation of outdated AI solutions.

Risk management is another critical aspect to consider when integrating AI into corporate communication strategies. Organizations must assess the potential risks associated with AI implementation, such as system failures, algorithmic errors, or reputational damage. Developing contingency plans and robust monitoring processes can help mitigate these risks and ensure a smooth integration of AI technology.

Finally, the human aspect must not be overlooked. As AI technology becomes more prevalent in corporate communication, concerns may arise about job displacement and the impact on the workforce. Organizations must address these concerns by providing reskilling and upskilling opportunities to employees, ensuring they can adapt to the changing landscape and continue to contribute value in an AI-driven environment.

Artificial Intelligence in Corporate Communication

In conclusion, while the integration of AI into corporate communication strategies presents numerous benefits, it also comes with its share of challenges and risks. By addressing data privacy concerns, mitigating bias, staying updated on AI advancements, managing risks, and prioritizing the human element, organizations can effectively navigate these challenges and leverage AI's transformative potential in corporate communication strategies.

Ethical Considerations in AI Adoption for Corporate Communication

As the AI revolution continues to reshape the corporate communication landscape, it is crucial for organizations to consider the ethical implications of integrating artificial intelligence into their communication strategies. While AI offers numerous benefits, such as improved efficiency, personalized messaging, and data-driven decision-making, it also raises important ethical considerations that must be addressed to ensure responsible and transparent use.

One key ethical concern in AI adoption for corporate communication is privacy and data protection. AI systems rely heavily on data to learn and make informed decisions. However, companies must ensure that they handle customer data in a secure and responsible manner, complying with applicable data protection regulations. Transparent data collection and usage practices, as well as obtaining informed consent from individuals, are essential to maintain trust and protect privacy rights.

Artificial Intelligence in Corporate Communication

Another ethical consideration is the potential for bias in AI algorithms. AI algorithms learn from existing data, which may contain biases inherent in society, such as gender or racial biases. These biases can inadvertently be perpetuated by AI systems, leading to discriminatory practices in corporate communication. It is crucial for organizations to regularly audit and monitor their AI systems to identify and address any biases, ensuring fair and unbiased communication practices.

Transparency and explainability are vital ethical considerations when adopting AI in corporate communication. AI systems often operate as black boxes, making it challenging to understand how they arrive at specific decisions or recommendations. Companies should strive to develop AI systems that can provide clear explanations for their actions, allowing stakeholders to understand and trust the decision-making process. Transparent AI systems foster accountability and avoid potential mistrust or suspicion.

Additionally, organizations must consider the potential impact of AI on human employees. While AI can automate certain communication tasks, it is essential to ensure that employees are not displaced or marginalized. Companies should focus on augmenting human capabilities with AI, promoting collaboration between humans and machines, and providing employees with the necessary training and upskilling opportunities to adapt to the changing landscape.

Lastly, ethical considerations in AI adoption require ongoing evaluation and adaptation. As AI technology evolves, new ethical challenges may arise.

Companies must remain vigilant, regularly reviewing their AI systems, and updating their policies and practices to align with ethical guidelines and societal expectations.

In conclusion, the adoption of AI in corporate communication brings immense potential. However, organizations must address ethical considerations to ensure responsible and transparent use. By prioritizing privacy and data protection, addressing biases, promoting transparency and explainability, considering the impact on employees, and continuously evaluating ethical implications, companies can harness the power of AI while maintaining trust and ethical integrity in their communication strategies.

Chapter 4: AI-powered Communication Tools and Technologies

Artificial Intelligence in Corporate Communication

Natural Language Processing (NLP) for Effective Communication

Artificial Intelligence in Corporate Communication

In today's fast-paced corporate environment, effective communication is crucial for success. With the advent of artificial intelligence (AI) and its integration into various aspects of business, the way we communicate is being redefined. One of the most significant advancements in AI is Natural Language Processing (NLP), which has revolutionized corporate communication strategies.

NLP is a branch of AI that focuses on the interaction between computers and human language. It enables machines to understand, interpret, and respond to human language in a way that mimics human intelligence. This technology has opened up new avenues for corporations to communicate more effectively with their stakeholders, customers, and employees.

One of the key benefits of NLP in corporate communication is its ability to analyze large volumes of data quickly and accurately. With the help of NLP algorithms, companies can process vast amounts of textual data, such as customer feedback, social media posts, and market research reports, to extract valuable insights. This allows businesses to gain a deeper understanding of their target audience, identify trends, and make data-driven decisions to improve their communication strategies.

Artificial Intelligence in Corporate Communication

NLP also plays a crucial role in automating routine communication tasks, freeing up valuable time for employees to focus on more strategic initiatives. Chatbots powered by NLP can handle customer queries, provide information, and resolve issues in real-time, providing a seamless and personalized experience. This not only enhances customer satisfaction but also improves operational efficiency.

Furthermore, NLP enables corporations to enhance their brand reputation and sentiment analysis. By analyzing social media conversations, online reviews, and news articles, companies can gauge public sentiment towards their brand and products. This information helps them identify potential issues and take proactive measures to address them, ultimately safeguarding their reputation.

Artificial Intelligence in Corporate Communication

The integration of NLP into corporate communication strategies has also made multilingual communication easier. With the ability to translate and understand multiple languages, NLP enables businesses to reach a global audience and expand their market reach. This is particularly valuable for multinational corporations that operate in diverse regions with different languages and cultural nuances.

In conclusion, Natural Language Processing (NLP) is transforming corporate communication strategies in the age of artificial intelligence. Its ability to analyze data, automate tasks, gauge sentiment, and facilitate multilingual communication has revolutionized the way businesses interact with their stakeholders.

Artificial Intelligence in Corporate Communication

As the AI revolution continues to reshape the corporate landscape, organizations that embrace NLP will gain a competitive edge by effectively communicating with their target audience and staying ahead of the game.

Chatbots and Virtual Assistants for Customer Engagement

Chatbots and virtual assistants have revolutionized the way businesses engage with their customers. In this subchapter, we will explore the immense potential of these AI-powered tools in enhancing customer engagement, and how they are redefining the game in corporate communication strategies.

Artificial Intelligence in Corporate Communication

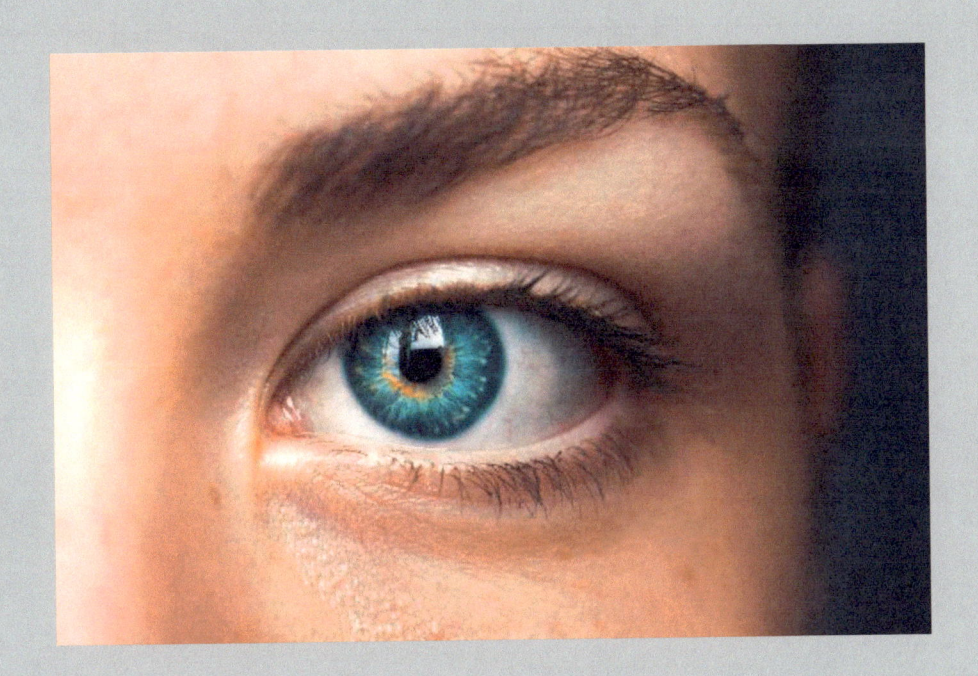

The AI revolution has impacted every aspect of corporate communication, and customer engagement is no exception. Chatbots and virtual assistants are intelligent systems that can interact with customers in a natural language format, providing them with instant support and information. These AI tools have become increasingly popular due to their ability to offer personalized and efficient customer service, available 24/7.

Artificial Intelligence in Corporate Communication

One of the key advantages of chatbots and virtual assistants is their ability to handle a large volume of customer queries simultaneously. Unlike human representatives, these AI tools don't experience fatigue or require breaks, ensuring uninterrupted customer support. This scalability allows businesses to cater to customer needs promptly, regardless of the time zone or geographical location.

Moreover, chatbots and virtual assistants can be seamlessly integrated into various communication channels, including websites, social media platforms, and messaging apps. This omnichannel presence enables businesses to engage with customers wherever they are, enhancing accessibility and convenience.

Artificial Intelligence in Corporate Communication

Furthermore, these AI-powered tools can collect and analyze vast amounts of customer data, providing invaluable insights into their preferences and behavior. By leveraging this information, businesses can create hyper-personalized marketing campaigns, improving customer satisfaction and loyalty. Chatbots and virtual assistants can also assist with lead generation, offering tailored recommendations and guiding customers through the sales funnel.

However, it is crucial for businesses to strike a balance between automation and human touch. While chatbots and virtual assistants are excellent at handling routine inquiries, complex or emotionally charged issues may still require human intervention. By seamlessly transitioning customers to human representatives when necessary, businesses can ensure a seamless and satisfying customer experience.

In conclusion, chatbots and virtual assistants are transforming customer engagement in corporate communication strategies. These AI-powered tools offer businesses the ability to provide instant, personalized, and scalable customer support, while also gathering valuable data for improved marketing strategies. By embracing the AI revolution, corporations can leverage chatbots and virtual assistants to redefine the game in customer engagement and gain a competitive edge in the market.

Speech Recognition and Voice Assistants in Corporate Communication

Speech recognition and voice assistants have revolutionized the way corporate communication strategies are implemented in today's fast-paced business environment. With the rise of artificial intelligence (AI), businesses are now capitalizing on the power of voice technology to enhance productivity, streamline operations, and improve customer experiences.

Artificial Intelligence in Corporate Communication

One of the key benefits of speech recognition in corporate communication lies in its ability to automate routine tasks. Voice assistants, powered by advanced AI algorithms, can transcribe meetings, emails, and other important documents accurately and in real-time. This eliminates the need for manual note-taking, allowing employees to focus on more strategic and value-added activities. Moreover, speech recognition technology can also be integrated with customer relationship management (CRM) systems, enabling efficient data entry and retrieval, and ensuring seamless collaboration across teams.

In addition to automation, voice assistants play a crucial role in enhancing employee productivity. With voice-enabled devices becoming increasingly popular, employees can now use voice commands to schedule meetings, set reminders, and access important information, all without needing to switch between different applications or devices. This hands-free approach not only saves time but also reduces distractions, allowing employees to concentrate on their core tasks. Furthermore, voice assistants can provide instant answers to common queries, acting as virtual assistants, and freeing up valuable time for employees.

Artificial Intelligence in Corporate Communication

In terms of customer communication, voice technology is transforming the way businesses interact with their clients. Voice assistants equipped with natural language processing (NLP) capabilities can understand customer queries and provide personalized responses, creating a more engaging and interactive experience. This not only enhances customer satisfaction but also enables businesses to gather valuable insights about their customers' preferences and behaviors.

However, while speech recognition and voice assistants offer numerous benefits, organizations need to address certain challenges as well. Data security and privacy concerns are of utmost importance, particularly when dealing with sensitive corporate information.

Artificial Intelligence in Corporate Communication

Robust security measures, such as encryption and authentication protocols, must be implemented to safeguard data integrity and prevent unauthorized access.

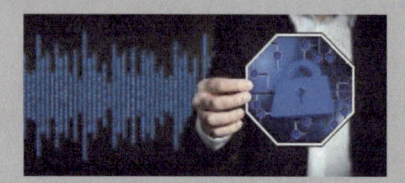

In conclusion, the integration of speech recognition and voice assistants into corporate communication strategies marks a significant milestone in the AI revolution. By leveraging these technologies, businesses can automate routine tasks, boost employee productivity, and enhance customer experiences.

However, it is crucial for organizations to address data security concerns to ensure the seamless and secure implementation of these powerful tools.

The era of voice-enabled corporate communication has arrived, and businesses that embrace it will undoubtedly redefine the game and gain a competitive edge in the market.

Redefining the Game

Artificial Intelligence in Corporate Communication

Sentiment Analysis and Emotion AI in Understanding Stakeholder Sentiments

In today's rapidly evolving corporate landscape, where communication strategies play a crucial role in shaping an organization's success, incorporating artificial intelligence (AI) has become imperative. One of the most impactful applications of AI in corporate communication is sentiment analysis and emotion AI, which helps organizations gain a deeper understanding of stakeholder sentiments.

Artificial Intelligence in Corporate Communication

Sentiment analysis leverages advanced natural language processing (NLP) algorithms to analyze text data and determine the emotional tone and sentiment expressed within it. By applying sentiment analysis to various communication channels such as social media, customer reviews, and employee surveys, corporations can gain real-time insights into stakeholder sentiments towards their brand, products, or services.

Emotion AI takes sentiment analysis a step further by attempting to understand and interpret human emotions. It uses machine learning algorithms to analyze non-verbal cues like facial expressions, tone of voice, and body language to gauge emotional states accurately. By integrating emotion AI into corporate communication strategies, organizations can derive invaluable insights into the emotions experienced by stakeholders during interactions, presentations, or product experiences.

Understanding stakeholder sentiments is crucial for corporations as it enables them to gauge the effectiveness of their communication strategies, identify areas for improvement, and tailor their messaging to resonate with their target audience. By utilizing sentiment analysis and emotion AI, corporations can navigate the complexities of today's business environment more effectively.

For example, sentiment analysis can help corporations monitor public sentiment towards their brand, allowing them to proactively address negative sentiment and capitalize on positive sentiment. By identifying and addressing customer pain points, corporations can enhance customer satisfaction, strengthen brand loyalty, and ultimately improve their bottom line.

Artificial Intelligence in Corporate Communication

Emotion AI can be particularly valuable during important presentations or interactions, allowing corporations to gauge the emotional responses of stakeholders in real-time. By analyzing the emotional states of stakeholders, organizations can adjust their communication style and content to ensure maximum impact. This can be particularly useful during product launches, negotiations, or team-building exercises.

In conclusion, the AI revolution in corporate communication strategies has made sentiment analysis and emotion AI indispensable tools for understanding stakeholder sentiments. By leveraging these technologies, corporations can gain valuable insights, refine their communication strategies, and foster stronger relationships with their stakeholders. Embracing AI in corporate communication is no longer an option but a necessity for organizations aiming to stay competitive in today's fast-paced business world.

Chapter 5: Leveraging AI for Internal Communication

Artificial Intelligence in Corporate Communication

AI-powered Employee Communication Platforms

In the fast-paced and technologically advanced world of corporate communication, businesses are constantly seeking innovative ways to streamline their internal communication processes. The advent of artificial intelligence (AI) has revolutionized the way companies communicate with their employees, paving the way for more efficient and effective employee communication platforms.

Artificial Intelligence in Corporate Communication

AI-powered employee communication platforms leverage the capabilities of AI to enhance internal communication within organizations. These platforms are designed to provide seamless communication channels, facilitate collaboration, and enable the dissemination of important information in real-time. By harnessing the power of AI, businesses can optimize their communication strategies and stay ahead in the competitive corporate landscape.

Artificial Intelligence in Corporate Communication

One of the key advantages of AI-powered employee communication platforms is their ability to automate routine tasks, saving valuable time and resources. These platforms can automatically sort and categorize messages, prioritize urgent communication, and even draft responses based on predefined templates. This not only improves efficiency but also allows employees to focus on more strategic and value-added tasks.

Furthermore, AI-powered platforms can analyze vast amounts of data generated from employee communication, providing valuable insights and trends. By leveraging natural language processing and machine learning algorithms, these platforms can identify sentiment, detect emerging issues, and even predict potential problems within the organization. This empowers businesses to proactively address concerns and enhance employee satisfaction, ultimately leading to improved productivity and performance.

In addition to streamlining communication processes, AI-powered platforms also foster collaboration and knowledge sharing among employees. These platforms can intelligently connect individuals with relevant expertise, making it easier for employees to find the right information or the right person to assist them. By breaking down silos and promoting cross-functional collaboration, businesses can leverage the collective intelligence of their workforce, driving innovation and problem-solving.

Artificial Intelligence in Corporate Communication

However, it is important to note that the successful implementation of AI-powered employee communication platforms requires careful planning and consideration. Companies need to ensure data privacy and security measures are in place to protect sensitive information. Additionally, organizations must provide adequate training and support to employees to effectively leverage the platform's capabilities.

The AI revolution in corporate communication strategies is reshaping the way businesses communicate with their employees. AI-powered employee communication platforms offer a multitude of benefits, from automating routine tasks to improving collaboration and knowledge sharing. By embracing these platforms, organizations can enhance their communication processes, boost employee engagement, and ultimately gain a competitive edge in the corporate world.

Redefining the Game

Artificial Intelligence in Corporate Communication

Personalized Employee Engagement and Feedback Systems

In the ever-evolving landscape of corporate communication strategies, the advent of artificial intelligence (AI) has ushered in a new era of personalized employee engagement and feedback systems.

As organizations strive to adapt to the AI revolution, incorporating these innovative technologies can redefine the game and revolutionize the way businesses interact with their workforce.

Artificial Intelligence in Corporate Communication

Gone are the days of one-size-fits-all approaches to employee engagement. With AI, companies can now create customized experiences tailored to each individual employee's needs, preferences, and goals. By leveraging machine learning algorithms, AI-powered systems can analyze vast amounts of data, including employee performance, feedback, and engagement metrics, to generate personalized recommendations and interventions.

Redefining the Game

One of the key benefits of personalized employee engagement systems is their ability to enhance employee motivation and job satisfaction. By understanding each employee's unique strengths, weaknesses, and interests, AI can suggest tailored learning and development opportunities, job rotations, or even career advancement paths. This not only increases employee engagement and productivity but also fosters a sense of loyalty and commitment to the organization.

Furthermore, AI-powered feedback systems enable real-time, continuous performance evaluations. Traditional annual or bi-annual performance reviews are often ineffective and fail to provide timely feedback. By implementing AI-driven feedback systems, managers can provide immediate feedback and recognition, allowing employees to make adjustments and improvements in real-time. This agile approach to feedback not only enhances employee performance but also facilitates a culture of continuous learning and growth.

Moreover, AI can help identify and address potential issues or conflicts within the workplace. By analyzing employee sentiment, communication patterns, and other relevant data, AI systems can detect early warning signs of disengagement, stress, or burnout. This proactive approach allows managers to intervene and provide support before these issues escalate, ultimately fostering a healthier and more positive work environment.

However, it is essential to strike a balance between personalized AI-driven systems and human interaction. While AI can provide valuable insights and recommendations, it should complement, rather than replace, human judgment and empathy. Encouraging open communication and maintaining a human touch in the employee engagement process will be crucial to building trust and ensuring the successful integration of AI technologies.

Artificial Intelligence in Corporate Communication

In conclusion, personalized employee engagement and feedback systems powered by AI are transforming corporate communication strategies. By leveraging the power of machine learning and data analytics, organizations can create tailored experiences that boost employee motivation, improve performance, and foster a culture of continuous learning. Embracing the AI revolution in corporate communication is not merely an option but a necessity for companies looking to stay competitive and drive sustainable growth in the modern business landscape.

AI-driven Knowledge Management and Collaboration Tools

In recent years, the corporate world has witnessed a transformative revolution driven by artificial intelligence (AI) technology. This revolution has permeated various aspects of business operations, and one area that has particularly benefited from AI is corporate communication strategies.

AI-driven knowledge management and collaboration tools have emerged as game-changers, enabling corporations to redefine the way they communicate and collaborate.

Knowledge management is crucial for any organization to thrive in today's fast-paced, information-driven world. Traditionally, managing vast amounts of data and knowledge has been a daunting task, often leading to inefficiencies and information silos.

However, with AI-driven knowledge management tools, corporations can now streamline their knowledge acquisition, organization, and dissemination processes. These tools employ machine learning algorithms to analyze vast amounts of data, extract relevant insights, and categorize information to ensure quick and efficient access.

Artificial Intelligence in Corporate Communication

Furthermore, AI-powered collaboration tools have revolutionized the way teams work together within an organization. Gone are the days of endless email chains and cumbersome file sharing processes. AI-driven collaboration tools enable seamless communication, real-time collaboration, and information sharing among team members. These tools leverage natural language processing (NLP) capabilities to facilitate efficient and effective communication, transcending geographical boundaries and time zones.

Artificial Intelligence in Corporate Communication

One of the key advantages of AI-driven knowledge management and collaboration tools is their ability to automate repetitive and time-consuming tasks. By automating mundane tasks such as data entry, content curation, and document management, employees can focus on more strategic and value-added activities. This not only boosts productivity but also enhances employee satisfaction and engagement.

Moreover, AI-driven tools can provide personalized recommendations and insights based on user behavior and preferences. By understanding individual employees' information needs and preferences, these tools can deliver tailored content and suggestions, improving knowledge sharing and decision-making processes within the organization.

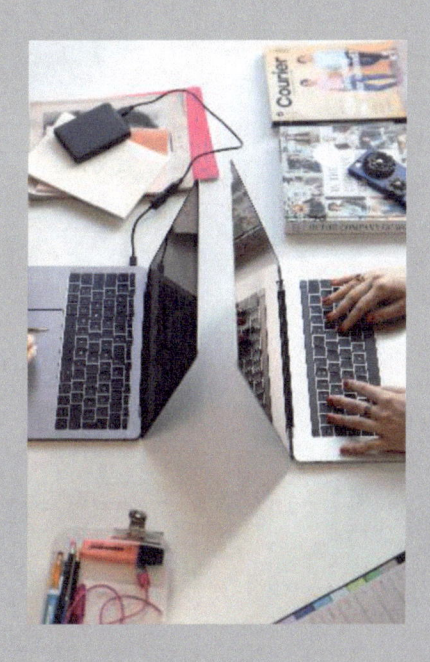

However, it is important for corporations to acknowledge the ethical considerations associated with AI-driven knowledge management and collaboration tools. Privacy, security, and bias are some of the critical concerns that need to be addressed to ensure responsible and ethical use of AI in corporate communication strategies.

In conclusion, AI-driven knowledge management and collaboration tools have revolutionized corporate communication strategies. These tools empower organizations to efficiently manage and share knowledge, enhance collaboration among teams, automate mundane tasks, and provide personalized insights. As the AI revolution continues to reshape the corporate landscape, embracing these tools will be vital for corporations to stay competitive and thrive in the digital age.

Chapter 6: AI-driven External Communication Strategies

AI-enhanced Customer Relationship Management (CRM)

Artificial Intelligence in Corporate Communication

In today's rapidly evolving business landscape, the integration of Artificial Intelligence (AI) has become crucial for corporate communication strategies. AI has revolutionized the way businesses interact with their customers, enabling them to provide personalized and seamless experiences. One area where AI has made a significant impact is in Customer Relationship Management (CRM), empowering companies to build stronger connections with their customers and drive long-term loyalty.

AI-enhanced CRM systems leverage the power of machine learning and natural language processing to intelligently analyze vast amounts of customer data. By tapping into this wealth of information, businesses can gain valuable insights into customer preferences, behaviors, and needs. This, in turn, enables companies to tailor their communication strategies to individual customers, fostering deeper engagement and enhancing the overall customer experience.

Artificial Intelligence in Corporate Communication

One of the most significant advantages of AI-enhanced CRM is its ability to automate routine tasks and streamline customer interactions. Chatbots, for example, are AI-powered virtual assistants that can handle customer inquiries and provide real-time support, 24/7. These intelligent bots can understand natural language, respond to queries, and even initiate proactive conversations with customers. By automating these processes, businesses can significantly reduce response times, enhance efficiency, and ultimately improve customer satisfaction.

Furthermore, AI-powered CRM systems can assist companies in predicting customer behavior patterns and identifying potential sales opportunities. By analyzing historical data, AI algorithms can anticipate future customer needs and preferences, enabling businesses to personalize their offerings and deliver targeted marketing campaigns. This predictive capability allows companies to stay one step ahead of customer demands and optimize their sales strategies accordingly.

Artificial Intelligence in Corporate Communication

Another critical aspect of AI-enhanced CRM is sentiment analysis. By analyzing social media posts, customer reviews, and other textual data, AI algorithms can determine the sentiment behind customer interactions. This valuable information allows businesses to gauge customer satisfaction levels, identify areas for improvement, and address potential issues promptly. By proactively addressing customer concerns, companies can enhance their reputation, build trust, and foster long-term customer loyalty.

In conclusion, AI-enhanced CRM is transforming the way corporate communication strategies are designed and executed. By leveraging the power of AI, businesses can gain valuable insights into customer behavior, automate routine tasks, and provide personalized experiences.

Artificial Intelligence in Corporate Communication

With AI-powered chatbots, predictive analytics, and sentiment analysis, companies can enhance customer satisfaction, build stronger relationships, and drive long-term business growth.

Embracing AI in CRM is no longer an option but a necessity for businesses aiming to stay competitive in the AI revolution in corporate communication strategies.

Redefining the Game

Artificial Intelligence in Corporate Communication

AI-powered Marketing and Advertising Campaigns

In the ever-evolving landscape of corporate communication strategies, Artificial Intelligence (AI) has emerged as a game-changer. With its ability to analyze vast amounts of data and make intelligent decisions, AI is revolutionizing the way companies approach marketing and advertising campaigns. This subchapter explores the impact of AI on marketing and advertising, and how it is reshaping the future of corporate communication.

Artificial Intelligence in Corporate Communication

AI-powered marketing campaigns leverage machine learning algorithms to deliver personalized and hyper-targeted content to customers. By analyzing customer behavior, preferences, and demographics, AI can create tailored messages that resonate with individual consumers. This level of personalization not only enhances customer experience but also drives higher conversion rates and customer loyalty.

One of the key benefits of AI in marketing and advertising is its ability to automate repetitive tasks. AI-powered chatbots and virtual assistants can handle customer inquiries, offer recommendations, and even process transactions, freeing up human resources to focus on more strategic initiatives. This automation not only improves efficiency but also ensures round-the-clock availability, enhancing customer satisfaction.

Artificial Intelligence in Corporate Communication

AI also plays a crucial role in deciphering complex consumer insights. By analyzing customer data from various sources, including social media, online behavior, and purchase history, AI can identify patterns and trends that human analysts may overlook. This deep understanding of consumer behavior enables companies to refine their advertising strategies and deliver highly relevant content that resonates with their target audience.

Artificial Intelligence in Corporate Communication

Furthermore, AI-powered marketing campaigns have the potential to optimize advertising spending. By analyzing historical data and real-time performance metrics, AI algorithms can identify the most effective channels, messages, and timing for ad placements. This data-driven decision-making ensures that companies invest their advertising budgets in the most impactful way, maximizing return on investment.

Artificial Intelligence in Corporate Communication

However, with the power of AI comes the responsibility to address ethical concerns. Companies must ensure transparency and accountability in their use of AI algorithms, safeguarding customer privacy and avoiding biased or discriminatory practices. Open dialogue and clear guidelines are essential to build trust and maintain ethical AI-powered marketing and advertising campaigns.

In conclusion, AI-powered marketing and advertising campaigns are transforming the corporate communication landscape. By harnessing the power of AI, companies can deliver personalized content, automate tasks, gain insights, and optimize advertising spending. However, it is essential for companies to navigate the ethical challenges associated with AI and prioritize transparency and accountability. The AI revolution in corporate communication strategies is here, and those who embrace it are well-positioned to redefine the game and stay ahead in the competitive business world.

Social Media and AI for Brand Reputation Management

In today's digital age, social media has become an integral part of our lives, transforming the way we communicate and interact with one another. With the rise of Artificial Intelligence (AI) technology, corporate communication strategies have been revolutionized, offering new opportunities for brand reputation management.

Social media platforms have provided businesses with a direct channel to connect and engage with their target audiences. However, this direct connection also exposes brands to potential reputation risks. Negative comments, viral misinformation, and online attacks can spread like wildfire, causing significant damage to a company's image and bottom line. This is where AI comes into play.

Artificial Intelligence in Corporate Communication

AI-powered tools and algorithms have the capability to monitor social media platforms in real-time, scanning for brand mentions, sentiment analysis, and potential reputation threats. By analyzing vast amounts of data, AI can identify patterns and trends, allowing corporate communication teams to swiftly respond to emerging issues and mitigate potential crises.

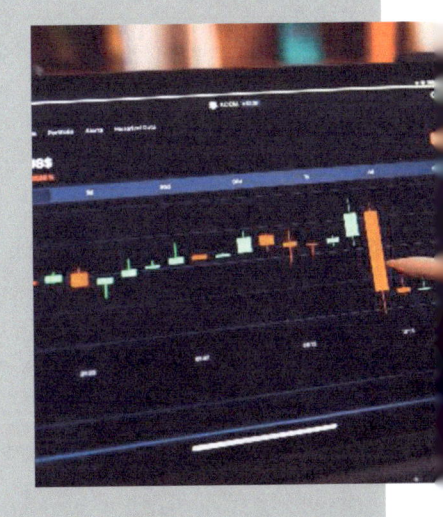

One of the key advantages of AI is its ability to provide instant feedback and insights. AI algorithms can analyze customer feedback, social media conversations, and online reviews to gain valuable insights into customer preferences, sentiment, and behavior.

Artificial Intelligence in Corporate Communication

This data can then be used to refine communication strategies, tailor messaging, and enhance brand reputation.

Furthermore, AI-powered chatbots have become increasingly popular in managing brand reputation on social media. These virtual assistants can provide real-time customer support, answer frequently asked questions, and address concerns promptly. By offering personalized and efficient customer service, chatbots not only improve customer satisfaction but also contribute to a positive brand image.

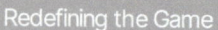

AI can also assist in tracking and analyzing influencers' impact on brand reputation. By using AI algorithms, brands can identify relevant influencers in their respective industries and collaborate with them to amplify positive brand messaging. AI algorithms can also assess influencers' credibility and authenticity, ensuring that brands partner with individuals who align with their values and objectives.

Artificial Intelligence in Corporate Communication

However, it is important to note that while AI can provide valuable insights and automate certain processes, it cannot replace human judgment and intuition. Corporate communication teams should work hand in hand with AI technologies, leveraging their capabilities to enhance brand reputation management strategies.

Artificial Intelligence in Corporate Communication

In conclusion, the integration of social media and AI in corporate communication strategies has revolutionized brand reputation management. AI-powered tools offer real-time monitoring, sentiment analysis, and crisis mitigation capabilities, enabling businesses to proactively address reputation threats. Additionally, AI provides valuable insights into customer preferences and behavior, allowing brands to refine their communication strategies. By embracing the power of AI and social media, corporate communication professionals can effectively navigate the ever-evolving digital landscape and ensure the longevity of their brands.

Artificial Intelligence in Corporate Communication

AI-enabled Public Relations and Crisis Communication

Artificial Intelligence in Corporate Communication

In the fast-paced world of corporate communication, staying ahead of the game is crucial. The advent of artificial intelligence (AI) has revolutionized the way companies approach their communication strategies, allowing them to adapt to the rapidly changing landscape. This subchapter delves into the realm of AI-enabled Public Relations (PR) and Crisis Communication, exploring how these technologies are reshaping the field.

In an era where information spreads like wildfire, companies need to be proactive in managing their public image. AI tools can analyze vast amounts of data from various sources, such as social media, news articles, and customer feedback, to monitor public sentiment towards a brand. By leveraging sentiment analysis algorithms, corporations can gain real-time insights into how they are perceived by the public, enabling them to fine-tune their PR strategies. AI-powered chatbots and virtual assistants have also become essential tools in customer service, allowing companies to provide instant responses and personalized experiences.

Artificial Intelligence in Corporate Communication

Moreover, AI has transformed crisis communication by enabling companies to respond swiftly and effectively during challenging times. Natural language processing algorithms can analyze social media posts, news articles, and other online content to identify emerging crises and potential reputation threats. This early warning system allows corporations to take proactive measures, mitigating the impact of such crises. AI can also assist in crafting crisis response messages by analyzing previous successful crisis communication cases, ensuring the delivery of consistent and appropriate messaging across various channels.

The incorporation of AI in PR and crisis communication presents both opportunities and challenges for corporate communication professionals. While AI streamlines many aspects of communication, it is imperative to strike a balance between human intuition and machine intelligence. The integration of AI should not replace human expertise, but rather enhance it. The role of PR professionals is still crucial in interpreting AI-generated insights and making strategic decisions based on their experience and understanding of the company's values.

Artificial Intelligence in Corporate Communication

In conclusion, the AI revolution is redefining corporate communication strategies, particularly in the domains of PR and crisis communication. By leveraging AI tools, companies can gain valuable insights into public sentiment, enhance customer service, and respond effectively during crises. However, it is essential for corporations to embrace AI as a complement to human expertise, ensuring that the human touch remains at the forefront. With the right balance, AI-enabled PR and crisis communication have the potential to revolutionize the way companies manage their public image and navigate through challenging times.

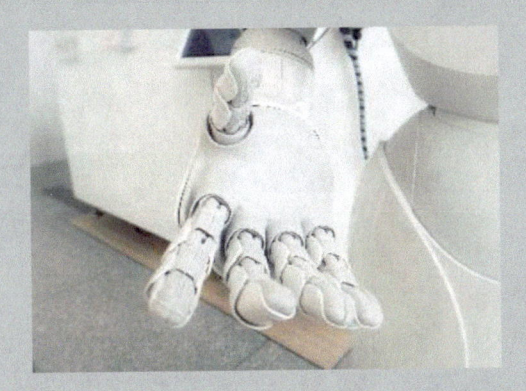

Chapter 7: The Future of Artificial Intelligence in Corporate Communication

Emerging Trends and Innovations in AI for Corporate Communication

The field of corporate communication is experiencing a rapid transformation due to the advancements in artificial intelligence (AI). Businesses across various industries are leveraging AI technologies to redefine their communication strategies and stay ahead in the game. This subchapter explores the emerging trends and innovations in AI for corporate communication, shedding light on the potential they hold for revolutionizing how businesses engage with their stakeholders.

Artificial Intelligence in Corporate Communication

One of the key trends in AI for corporate communication is the use of chatbots and virtual assistants. These intelligent systems are capable of understanding and responding to natural language, allowing organizations to automate customer interactions and provide real-time support. Chatbots can be integrated into websites, social media platforms, and messaging apps, enabling businesses to deliver personalized and efficient communication at scale.

Artificial Intelligence in Corporate Communication

Another significant trend is the application of AI in sentiment analysis and reputation management. By analyzing vast amounts of data from social media, news articles, and customer feedback, AI-powered tools can gauge public sentiment towards a brand or product. This information helps businesses proactively address any negative sentiment and make data-driven decisions to enhance their reputation and brand image.

Artificial Intelligence in Corporate Communication

AI is also being utilized for content generation and curation. Natural language processing algorithms can generate high-quality content, such as news articles, reports, and social media posts, with minimal human intervention. Moreover, AI algorithms can curate personalized content recommendations for individual stakeholders based on their preferences and behavior, ensuring that the right message reaches the right audience at the right time.

The integration of AI with data analytics is another emerging trend in corporate communication. AI algorithms can analyze large datasets to identify patterns, trends, and insights that can be used to optimize communication strategies. By leveraging AI-powered analytics, businesses can gain a deeper understanding of their target audience, predict their needs, and tailor their communication accordingly.

Furthermore, AI is revolutionizing the field of crisis communication. Intelligent systems can monitor online conversations and news articles in real-time, alerting organizations to potential crises and enabling them to respond promptly. AI can also provide valuable insights into the effectiveness of crisis communication strategies, helping businesses learn from past experiences and improve their crisis response tactics.

Artificial Intelligence in Corporate Communication

In conclusion, the emergence of AI in corporate communication is reshaping how businesses engage with their stakeholders. From chatbots and sentiment analysis to content generation and crisis communication, AI technologies offer immense potential for enhancing communication strategies in the corporate world. Embracing these emerging trends and innovations is crucial for businesses to stay competitive and navigate the ever-evolving landscape of corporate communication in the AI era.

Impact of AI on Job Roles and Skills in Corporate Communication

In the rapidly evolving world of business, the integration of artificial intelligence (AI) has become inevitable. As companies strive to stay ahead of the competition and meet the ever-changing needs of their customers, AI has emerged as a game-changer in corporate communication strategies.

This subchapter explores the profound impact of AI on job roles and skills within the corporate communication sector.

Artificial Intelligence in Corporate Communication

One of the most prominent effects of AI in corporate communication is the transformation of job roles. Traditional positions such as public relations specialists, content creators, and social media managers are being reshaped by AI technologies. AI-powered chatbots are now capable of handling basic customer inquiries, reducing the need for human customer service representatives. This shift allows professionals to focus on more complex tasks that require human intuition, creativity, and critical thinking.

Redefining the Game

Artificial Intelligence in Corporate Communication

Skills required in corporate communication are also evolving due to AI integration. While technical skills such as data analysis, programming, and machine learning are increasingly in demand, soft skills like emotional intelligence, adaptability, and collaboration are becoming equally important. The ability to understand and work alongside AI technologies is crucial for professionals in this field. Effective communication with AI systems, interpreting and utilizing AI-generated insights, and making sound decisions based on AI recommendations are becoming essential skills for corporate communication professionals.

Artificial Intelligence in Corporate Communication

Moreover, AI is enabling professionals to streamline their work processes and achieve greater efficiency. AI-powered tools can automate repetitive tasks, analyze vast amounts of data, and provide valuable insights for decision-making. This allows corporate communication teams to allocate their time and resources more effectively, focusing on strategic planning, relationship building, and creative problem-solving.

However, the integration of AI also brings challenges. As AI technologies become more advanced, concerns arise about job displacement and the future of human work. It is crucial for organizations to foster a culture of continuous learning and upskilling to ensure that employees can adapt to the changing landscape. Developing a hybrid workforce that combines the unique capabilities of AI with human expertise will be vital for success in the AI revolution.

Artificial Intelligence in Corporate Communication

In conclusion, the impact of AI on job roles and skills in corporate communication is profound. While certain positions may undergo transformation or even disappear, new opportunities for professionals with the right skillset are emerging. The integration of AI in corporate communication strategies requires individuals to acquire a mix of technical and soft skills to effectively collaborate with AI technologies. By embracing AI and fostering continuous learning, corporate communication professionals can harness the potential of AI to redefine the game and stay competitive in the ever-evolving business landscape.

Artificial Intelligence in Corporate Communication

Ethical and Legal Implications of AI Adoption in Corporate Communication

In recent years, the corporate world has witnessed a significant shift in communication strategies, thanks to the rapid advancements in artificial intelligence (AI) technology. This subchapter explores the ethical and legal implications that arise with the adoption of AI in corporate communication, shedding light on the need for responsible and transparent practices.

One of the key ethical concerns surrounding AI adoption in corporate communication is the potential for bias. AI algorithms are trained using vast amounts of data, and if this data contains biased information, it can lead to discriminatory outcomes. For instance, if an AI-powered chatbot is used as a customer service representative, it may unintentionally display bias in its responses, leading to unequal treatment of customers. Corporations need to ensure that their AI systems are regularly audited to identify and rectify any biases that emerge.

Artificial Intelligence in Corporate Communication

Another ethical consideration is the impact of AI on employment. As AI technology continues to advance, there is a fear that it will replace human workers, leading to job losses. Organizations must carefully consider the ethical implications of implementing AI systems, taking measures to reskill or redeploy employees affected by automation. This will help maintain a fair and inclusive work environment.

In addition to ethical concerns, legal implications also arise with AI adoption in corporate communication. Data privacy is a critical issue that must be addressed. AI systems often rely on collecting and analyzing vast amounts of personal data, raising concerns about the misuse or unauthorized access to sensitive information. Corporations must ensure that they comply with relevant data protection regulations and establish robust security measures to safeguard user data.

Artificial Intelligence in Corporate Communication

Transparency is another legal consideration. Organizations need to clearly communicate to their stakeholders that they are using AI systems in their communication processes. This transparency will build trust and help manage potential legal challenges that may arise due to the use of AI.

To navigate these ethical and legal implications successfully, corporations must adopt a proactive approach. This involves developing AI governance frameworks that outline responsible and ethical use of the technology.

Artificial Intelligence in Corporate Communication

Regular audits should be conducted to identify and address biases, and employees should be provided with training on AI ethics. Additionally, collaboration with legal experts and regulators will help ensure compliance with relevant laws and regulations.

In conclusion, while AI adoption in corporate communication offers numerous benefits, it also comes with ethical and legal considerations. By adhering to responsible practices, organizations can harness the power of AI while maintaining fairness, transparency, and compliance.

Chapter 8: Best Practices for Implementing AI in Corporate Communication

Understanding the Organizational Context and Objectives

In the fast-paced and ever-evolving corporate world, the role of artificial intelligence (AI) in communication strategies has become increasingly significant. This subchapter aims to provide corporate professionals with a deeper understanding of the organizational context and objectives when incorporating AI into their communication practices.

Artificial Intelligence in Corporate Communication

The AI revolution in corporate communication strategies has transformed the way organizations interact with their stakeholders. AI-powered tools and technologies have enabled companies to streamline their communication processes, enhance customer experiences, and analyze vast amounts of data to make informed decisions. However, to harness the full potential of AI, it is crucial to comprehend the organizational context and objectives that drive its implementation.

Artificial Intelligence in Corporate Communication

First and foremost, organizations need to assess their communication needs and objectives. Understanding the specific challenges and opportunities faced by the company will help identify areas where AI can make a real difference. Whether it is improving internal communication, enhancing customer engagement, or optimizing social media campaigns, aligning AI initiatives with the organization's strategic goals is essential.

Furthermore, organizations must consider their existing technological infrastructure and resources. Integrating AI into corporate communication strategies requires a robust technological foundation that supports data collection, processing, and analysis. Assessing the organization's readiness for AI implementation will provide insights into the necessary upgrades, investments, or collaborations required to leverage AI effectively.

Another critical aspect to consider is the potential impact of AI on the workforce. While AI can automate routine tasks and improve efficiency, it may also disrupt certain job roles. Organizations must proactively address employee concerns and provide training and reskilling opportunities to ensure a smooth transition. By embracing AI as a complement to human capabilities, organizations can create a collaborative and innovative work environment.

Artificial Intelligence in Corporate Communication

Moreover, understanding the ethical implications of AI is paramount. Corporate professionals must consider the ethical frameworks and guidelines when designing AI-powered communication strategies. Ensuring transparency, privacy, and fairness in AI implementation is vital to maintain trust and credibility with stakeholders.

In conclusion, understanding the organizational context and objectives is crucial for the successful integration of AI into corporate communication strategies. By aligning AI initiatives with strategic goals, assessing technological readiness, addressing the workforce impact, and adhering to ethical considerations, organizations can leverage AI to redefine the game of corporate communication. Embracing the AI revolution will enable companies to stay ahead in a competitive landscape and deliver exceptional experiences to their stakeholders.

Artificial Intelligence in Corporate Communication

Developing a Comprehensive AI Strategy

In today's rapidly evolving business landscape, the integration of artificial intelligence (AI) has become paramount to staying competitive. As corporate communication strategies face the disruptive force of the AI revolution, organizations need to develop comprehensive AI strategies to redefine their game and ensure their long-term success.

Artificial Intelligence in Corporate Communication

The AI revolution in corporate communication strategies is transforming the way businesses interact with their customers, employees, and stakeholders. AI-powered technologies such as chatbots, natural language processing, and machine learning have opened up new avenues for personalized and efficient communication. From automating repetitive tasks to analyzing vast amounts of data, AI enables organizations to streamline their communication processes and make data-driven decisions.

Artificial Intelligence in Corporate Communication

Developing a comprehensive AI strategy requires a holistic approach that aligns AI initiatives with organizational goals and values. It begins with a thorough assessment of the current communication landscape, identifying pain points, and areas where AI can add value. Understanding the specific needs and challenges of the organization will facilitate the selection and implementation of AI technologies that are most suitable for achieving its objectives.

Artificial Intelligence in Corporate Communication

To develop an effective AI strategy, corporate leaders must foster a culture of innovation and embrace a mindset that encourages experimentation. This involves investing in research and development, collaborating with AI experts, and staying abreast of the latest advancements in AI technology. By creating an environment that fosters curiosity and continuous learning, organizations can unlock the full potential of AI and drive transformative change in their communication strategies.

It is crucial to acknowledge that AI is not a one-size-fits-all solution. Organizations must carefully consider the ethical implications and potential risks associated with AI deployment. They must establish robust governance frameworks and ensure transparency, fairness, and accountability in AI-driven communication processes. By doing so, corporations can build trust with their stakeholders and maintain ethical standards while reaping the benefits of AI.

Furthermore, organizations need to invest in the development and upskilling of their workforce to adapt to the AI revolution. By providing training programs and resources, corporations can empower their employees to leverage AI technologies and enhance their communication capabilities. This not only enables seamless collaboration between humans and AI but also fosters a culture of innovation and agility within the organization.

Artificial Intelligence in Corporate Communication

In conclusion, developing a comprehensive AI strategy is imperative for corporations to navigate the AI revolution in corporate communication strategies successfully. By aligning AI initiatives with organizational goals, fostering a culture of innovation, addressing ethical considerations, and investing in employee development, organizations can redefine the game and stay ahead in the rapidly evolving business landscape. Embracing AI as a strategic ally will empower corporations to revolutionize their communication practices and unlock new opportunities for growth and success.

Artificial Intelligence in Corporate Communication

Addressing Employee Concerns and Ensuring Ethical AI Practices

As the AI revolution continues to reshape corporate communication strategies, it is crucial for organizations to address employee concerns and establish ethical AI practices. While AI has the potential to greatly enhance efficiency and productivity, it also raises important ethical considerations that must be carefully navigated to ensure the well-being of employees and maintain trust within the organization.

One of the primary concerns employees may have is the fear of job displacement. AI technologies, such as chatbots and automated systems, have the ability to handle routine tasks and streamline workflows, potentially reducing the need for certain roles. It is essential for organizations to communicate transparently with employees about the intended use of AI and how it will impact their roles. This involves providing reassurance that AI is meant to complement human capabilities rather than replace them, and that it will free up employees to focus on more strategic and value-added tasks.

Another crucial aspect is ensuring the ethical use of AI. Organizations must establish clear guidelines and policies to prevent AI from being used in ways that could compromise privacy, security, or fairness. This includes addressing potential biases in AI algorithms and regularly auditing and monitoring AI systems to identify and rectify any ethical issues that may arise. Additionally, organizations should actively involve employees in the development and implementation of AI systems, seeking their input and ensuring their concerns are heard and addressed.

Artificial Intelligence in Corporate Communication

Training and upskilling employees is also vital in the AI era. By providing opportunities for employees to learn and develop new skills that are in demand in the AI-driven workplace, organizations can empower their workforce to adapt and thrive amidst the changing landscape. This can help alleviate concerns about job displacement and foster a culture of continuous learning and growth within the organization.

Artificial Intelligence in Corporate Communication

Furthermore, organizations should establish channels for employees to voice their concerns and provide feedback regarding AI technologies. This can be done through regular town hall meetings, surveys, or dedicated platforms where employees can anonymously share their thoughts and experiences. By actively listening to employee concerns and taking appropriate actions, organizations can demonstrate their commitment to creating an inclusive and ethical AI-driven workplace.

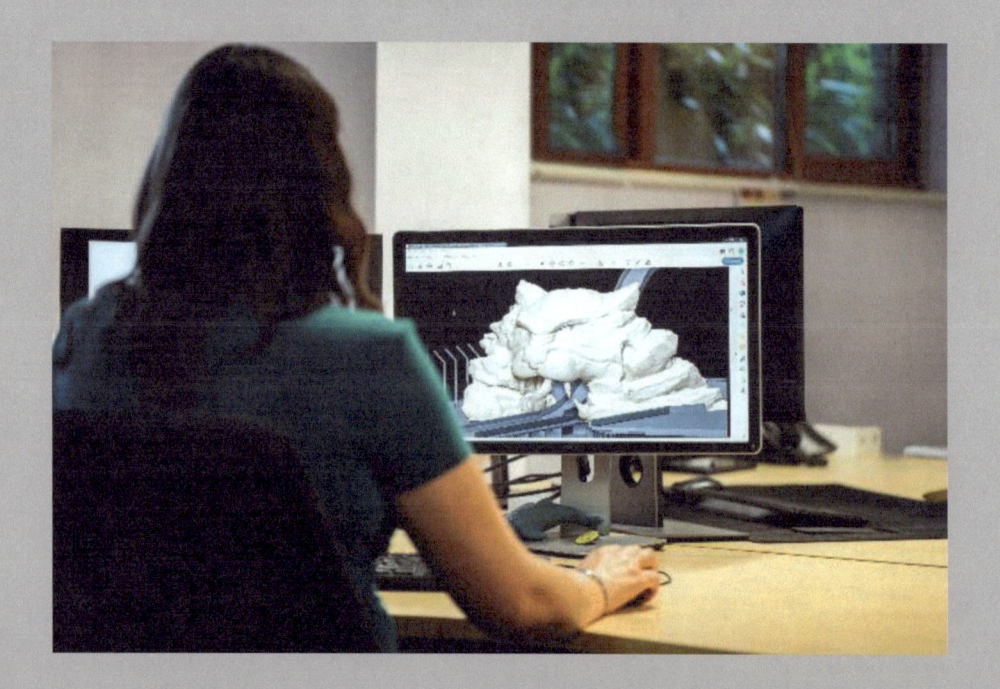

In conclusion, addressing employee concerns and ensuring ethical AI practices are crucial for organizations navigating the AI revolution in corporate communication strategies. By transparently communicating the role of AI, establishing ethical guidelines, providing training and upskilling opportunities, and fostering a culture of open communication, organizations can build trust, empower their employees, and navigate the AI revolution successfully.

Artificial Intelligence in Corporate Communication

Evaluating and Measuring the Effectiveness of AI-driven Communication

Artificial Intelligence in Corporate Communication

In the rapidly evolving landscape of corporate communication, the integration of artificial intelligence (AI) has revolutionized the way organizations interact with their stakeholders. As AI continues to reshape communication strategies, it becomes imperative for corporate entities to evaluate and measure the effectiveness of AI-driven communication initiatives.

Measuring the effectiveness of AI-driven communication is crucial for organizations to understand the impact of their efforts and optimize their strategies accordingly. One of the primary metrics to evaluate is the level of engagement generated through AI-driven communication channels. By analyzing the number of interactions, responses, and conversions, corporations can gauge the effectiveness of their AI systems in capturing and retaining the attention of their target audience.

Furthermore, sentiment analysis plays a vital role in evaluating the success of AI-driven communication. Tracking and analyzing the sentiment expressed by stakeholders through AI-powered chatbots, virtual assistants, or automated customer service systems can provide valuable insights into their satisfaction levels. Corporations can leverage these insights to enhance their communication strategies, identify areas of improvement, and address any concerns promptly.

Artificial Intelligence in Corporate Communication

In addition to engagement and sentiment analysis, corporations should also assess the efficiency and accuracy of AI-driven communication systems. Evaluating response times, problem-solving capabilities, and the accuracy of information provided by AI systems can help organizations identify bottlenecks and ensure the effectiveness of their communication channels.

Moreover, organizations need to measure the impact of AI-driven communication on their overall business goals. This involves analyzing key performance indicators (KPIs) such as lead generation, customer acquisition, and revenue growth. By tracking these metrics, corporations can determine the direct impact of AI-driven communication initiatives and make data-driven decisions to optimize their strategies.

To effectively evaluate and measure the effectiveness of AI-driven communication, corporations should leverage advanced analytics tools and technologies. These tools can provide comprehensive insights into customer behavior, preferences, and patterns, helping organizations fine-tune their AI systems and achieve better outcomes.

In conclusion, evaluating and measuring the effectiveness of AI-driven communication is essential for corporations in the era of the AI revolution.

By analyzing metrics such as engagement, sentiment, efficiency, and impact on business goals, organizations can optimize their communication strategies and drive better results.

Embracing advanced analytics tools and technologies will enable corporations to stay ahead of the game and leverage the power of AI in corporate communication.

Chapter 9: Case Studies: Successful AI Integration in Corporate Communication

Case Study 1: Company X – Leveraging AI for Internal Communication

Artificial Intelligence in Corporate Communication

Subchapter 1: Case Study 1: Company X - Leveraging AI for Internal Communication

In today's rapidly evolving business landscape, companies across industries are realizing the immense potential of Artificial Intelligence (AI) in transforming their communication strategies. One such company that stands out is Company X, a leading player in the corporate world. Through its innovative approach to internal communication, Company X has successfully harnessed AI to redefine its communication game, resulting in improved efficiency, collaboration, and employee engagement.

Artificial Intelligence in Corporate Communication

Company X recognized the need to adapt to the AI revolution in corporate communication strategies to stay ahead of the competition. By leveraging AI-powered tools and platforms, they have managed to streamline their internal communication processes and enhance overall organizational effectiveness.

One of the key aspects of Company X's approach is the implementation of AI chatbots. By integrating AI chatbots into their internal communication channels, employees can quickly access relevant information, resolve queries, and receive real-time updates. These chatbots, powered by natural language processing and machine learning, have significantly reduced the time and effort required for employees to find the information they need, thus improving productivity and eliminating communication bottlenecks.

Furthermore, Company X has employed sentiment analysis algorithms to gain insights into employee sentiments and engagement levels. By analyzing text data from various communication channels such as emails, chat logs, and surveys, they can identify patterns and trends, enabling them to proactively address any issues or concerns. This AI-driven approach has fostered a more inclusive and supportive work environment, leading to increased employee satisfaction and retention.

Artificial Intelligence in Corporate Communication

Additionally, Company X has utilized AI-powered virtual assistants to enhance collaboration and project management. These virtual assistants can schedule meetings, set reminders, and provide real-time status updates on ongoing projects. By automating routine tasks, employees can focus on more value-added activities, leading to improved efficiency and productivity.

The success of Company X in leveraging AI for internal communication can be attributed to their commitment to innovation and their understanding of the evolving corporate communication landscape. By embracing AI technologies, they have redefined their communication game, ensuring a competitive edge in the market.

Artificial Intelligence in Corporate Communication

This case study serves as a testament to the transformative potential of AI in corporate communication strategies. As the AI revolution continues to reshape the business landscape, it is crucial for companies to adapt and leverage AI tools and platforms to optimize their internal communication processes, foster collaboration, and drive organizational success.

Artificial Intelligence in Corporate Communication

Case Study 2: Company Y - AI-powered Customer Engagement Strategies

In this subchapter, we will delve into a fascinating case study that showcases the power of AI in revolutionizing customer engagement strategies.

Company Y, a leading player in the corporate communication space, has successfully harnessed the potential of AI to enhance its customer interactions and deliver personalized experiences at scale.

As the AI revolution continues to reshape corporate communication strategies, Company Y recognized the need to leverage AI-powered solutions to stay competitive and meet the evolving demands of its customer base. By adopting AI technologies, they aimed to improve customer engagement, drive brand loyalty, and ultimately enhance their bottom line.

Artificial Intelligence in Corporate Communication

To begin their transformation, Company Y employed AI algorithms to analyze vast amounts of customer data from various touchpoints, such as social media, email interactions, and website behavior. This allowed them to gain deeper insights into their customers' preferences, needs, and behavior patterns. Armed with this information, they could tailor their communication strategies to target specific customer segments and deliver more relevant content.

One of the key AI-powered initiatives implemented by Company Y was the use of chatbots for customer support. By integrating natural language processing and machine learning algorithms, these chatbots could handle customer queries in real-time, providing instant responses and resolutions. This not only reduced customer wait times but also improved overall customer satisfaction.

Artificial Intelligence in Corporate Communication

Moreover, Company Y leveraged AI to develop personalized recommendations and product suggestions. By analyzing customer purchase history, browsing behavior, and demographic data, AI algorithms could predict and recommend relevant products or services to individual customers. This personalized approach enhanced the customer experience, leading to increased sales and higher customer retention rates.

Additionally, AI-powered sentiment analysis enabled Company Y to monitor and gauge customer sentiments towards their brand in real-time. By analyzing social media conversations, customer reviews, and other online interactions, they could identify potential issues or concerns and proactively address them. This proactive approach helped in building a positive brand image and fostering strong customer relationships.

Artificial Intelligence in Corporate Communication

In conclusion, Company Y's successful integration of AI-powered customer engagement strategies has transformed how they communicate with their customers. By leveraging AI to analyze customer data, deploy chatbots, provide personalized recommendations, and monitor sentiments, they have redefined customer engagement in the corporate communication landscape. This case study exemplifies the immense potential AI holds in reshaping corporate communication strategies, enabling companies to deliver exceptional customer experiences and drive business growth.

Case Study 3: Company Z - AI-driven Crisis Communication Management

In the fast-paced world of corporate communication, the ability to effectively manage crises is paramount. In this case study, we will explore how Company Z leveraged artificial intelligence (AI) to redefine their crisis communication strategies.

Company Z, a leading player in the telecommunications industry, faced a major crisis when a security breach compromised sensitive customer data. The incident attracted significant media attention and threatened to tarnish the company's reputation.

Recognizing the need for swift and effective crisis communication, Company Z turned to AI to navigate this challenging situation.

Artificial Intelligence in Corporate Communication

With the help of AI-powered analytics tools, Company Z was able to swiftly identify the most relevant information from the vast amount of data generated by the crisis. These tools provided real-time monitoring of news articles, social media platforms, and customer feedback, enabling the company to stay on top of the rapidly evolving situation. AI algorithms analyzed sentiment and detected patterns in the data, allowing Company Z to anticipate potential negative reactions and respond proactively.

Artificial Intelligence in Corporate Communication

By understanding public sentiment, they were able to tailor their crisis communication messages accordingly, ensuring that their responses resonated with their target audience.

Moreover, AI-powered chatbots became a fundamental component of the crisis communication strategy. These chatbots were trained to handle a wide range of customer queries and concerns related to the breach, providing instant responses and reassurance. By automating these interactions, Company Z was able to scale their crisis communication efforts, handling a large volume of inquiries efficiently and effectively.

The use of AI also enabled Company Z to personalize their crisis communication efforts. By leveraging data on individual customer preferences and communication channels, the company delivered tailored messages to affected customers, addressing their concerns and offering personalized support. This personal touch helped restore customer confidence and mitigate the negative impact of the crisis.

Company Z's AI-driven crisis communication management approach not only allowed them to navigate the security breach effectively but also strengthened their overall corporate communication strategies. By harnessing the power of AI, they were able to identify potential crises early on, respond promptly, and ensure consistent messaging across different communication channels.

Artificial Intelligence in Corporate Communication

This case study illustrates the transformative potential of AI in revolutionizing corporate communication strategies. By leveraging AI technologies, companies can proactively manage crises, engage with customers more effectively, and safeguard their reputation in an increasingly complex and interconnected world. Embracing the AI revolution in corporate communication is no longer an option but a necessity for companies seeking to stay ahead in the competitive landscape.

Chapter 10: Conclusion

Artificial Intelligence in Corporate Communication

Recap of Key Learnings

In this subchapter, we will summarize the key learnings from the book "Artificial Intelligence in Corporate Communication: Redefining the Game" and highlight the crucial insights that corporate professionals can apply to leverage the AI revolution in their communication strategies.

Artificial Intelligence in Corporate Communication

1. Understanding the AI Revolution:
First and foremost, the book emphasizes the significance of comprehending the AI revolution and its implications on corporate communication strategies. It explains how AI technologies such as natural language processing, machine learning, and chatbots are reshaping the way organizations interact with their stakeholders.

2. Harnessing Data for Insights:
One of the key takeaways is the importance of utilizing data-driven insights to enhance corporate communication efforts. The book delves into how AI enables corporations to analyze vast amounts of data, extract meaningful patterns, and leverage these insights to make informed decisions, enhance customer experiences, and drive organizational growth.

3. Personalization and Customization:
The AI revolution presents an opportunity for corporations to personalize and customize their communication strategies. By harnessing AI-powered tools, organizations can tailor their messaging to individual stakeholders, increasing engagement and building stronger relationships. The book provides practical examples and case studies to illustrate how personalization can lead to improved business outcomes.

4. Chatbots and Virtual Assistants:

Another crucial learning from the book is the potential of chatbots and virtual assistants in corporate communication. It explores how AI-powered chatbots can effectively handle routine customer queries, provide instant support, and free up human resources for more complex tasks. The book also highlights the need to strike a balance between automation and human interaction to ensure a seamless customer experience.

5. Ethical Considerations:

The ethical implications of AI in corporate communication are vital to understand. The book emphasizes the need for responsible AI adoption, considering factors like privacy, security, and bias. It encourages corporations to develop robust ethical guidelines and frameworks to ensure AI technologies are used ethically and transparently.

In conclusion, "Artificial Intelligence in Corporate Communication: Redefining the Game" provides valuable insights and practical guidance for corporate professionals seeking to leverage the AI revolution in their communication strategies. By understanding the AI revolution, harnessing data for insights, personalizing communication, leveraging chatbots, and considering ethical implications, corporations can redefine their communication game and stay ahead in the ever-evolving corporate landscape.

Artificial Intelligence in Corporate Communication

Redefining the Game

Final Thoughts on the Future of AI in Corporate Communication

As we conclude this captivating journey exploring the impact of Artificial Intelligence (AI) in corporate communication, it is crucial to reflect on the future possibilities and potential that lie ahead. The AI revolution has undoubtedly unleashed a new era of innovation and transformation in corporate communication strategies, presenting both opportunities and challenges for organizations of all sizes and industries.

The integration of AI technologies has already demonstrated its value in corporate communication, enabling businesses to streamline processes, enhance efficiency, and deliver more personalized and targeted messaging. From chatbots that provide instant customer support to automated content creation and sentiment analysis, AI has proven to be a game-changer in the way companies communicate with their stakeholders.

Artificial Intelligence in Corporate Communication

Looking ahead, the future of AI in corporate communication holds endless possibilities. As AI technology advances, we can expect even more sophisticated applications that will push the boundaries of what is currently imaginable. For instance, AI-powered virtual assistants may become commonplace, seamlessly handling tasks such as scheduling meetings, organizing emails, and even drafting communication materials.

Redefining the Game

Moreover, AI can revolutionize the way organizations analyze and interpret big data. The ability to gather, process, and analyze vast amounts of information in real-time will undoubtedly empower companies to make data-driven decisions and uncover valuable insights that can drive business growth and competitive advantage.

However, as we embrace the potential of AI in corporate communication, it is crucial to acknowledge and address the challenges it poses. Ethical considerations surrounding data privacy, algorithm bias, and job displacement need to be carefully navigated to ensure that AI is used responsibly and in the best interest of all stakeholders.

In conclusion, the AI revolution in corporate communication strategies is reshaping the future of business communication. As AI technologies continue to evolve, organizations must remain agile and adapt their communication strategies to leverage the benefits offered by AI while mitigating potential risks. By embracing AI as a powerful tool, businesses can enhance their communication effectiveness, strengthen customer relationships, and gain a competitive edge in an increasingly digital and interconnected world.

Artificial Intelligence in Corporate Communication

The time to embrace the AI revolution in corporate communication is now. The future holds tremendous potential, and organizations that proactively incorporate AI into their communication strategies will be at the forefront of the next wave of innovation and success. Let us embark on this exciting journey together and redefine the game of corporate communication through the power of AI.

Closing Remarks

In the fast-paced world of corporate communication, the advent of artificial intelligence (AI) has undoubtedly redefined the game. As we reach the end of this book, "Artificial Intelligence in Corporate Communication: Redefining the Game," it is important to reflect on the transformative impact of AI on corporate communication strategies and the broader implications it holds for businesses in today's AI revolution.

Throughout this book, we have explored the various applications of AI in corporate communication, delving into its potential to streamline processes, enhance customer experiences, and drive business growth. We have witnessed how AI-powered chatbots have revolutionized customer service, providing real-time support and personalized interactions, thereby elevating customer satisfaction to new heights.

We have also discussed how AI analytics and sentiment analysis have empowered companies to gain valuable insights into customer behavior, enabling them to tailor their communication strategies more effectively.

Artificial Intelligence in Corporate Communication

The AI revolution in corporate communication strategies is not just about technological advancements; it is a paradigm shift in how we communicate with customers, employees, and stakeholders.

It calls for a shift in mindset, embracing the potential of AI to augment human capabilities rather than replacing them. As the AI landscape continues to evolve, it is crucial for corporate leaders and communication professionals to adapt and stay ahead of the curve.

Moreover, it is imperative to address the ethical implications surrounding AI integration in corporate communication. As AI becomes more integral to our communication strategies, we must ensure that ethical considerations are at the forefront. This includes transparency, accountability, and safeguarding user privacy. By adhering to ethical frameworks, businesses can build trust with their stakeholders and foster long-term relationships.

Artificial Intelligence in Corporate Communication

The journey towards maximizing the potential of AI in corporate communication is ongoing. It requires continuous learning, experimentation, and collaboration. As corporate professionals, we must embrace this revolution and seize the opportunities it presents. By harnessing the power of AI, we can redefine corporate communication practices, drive innovation, and gain a competitive edge in today's digital landscape.

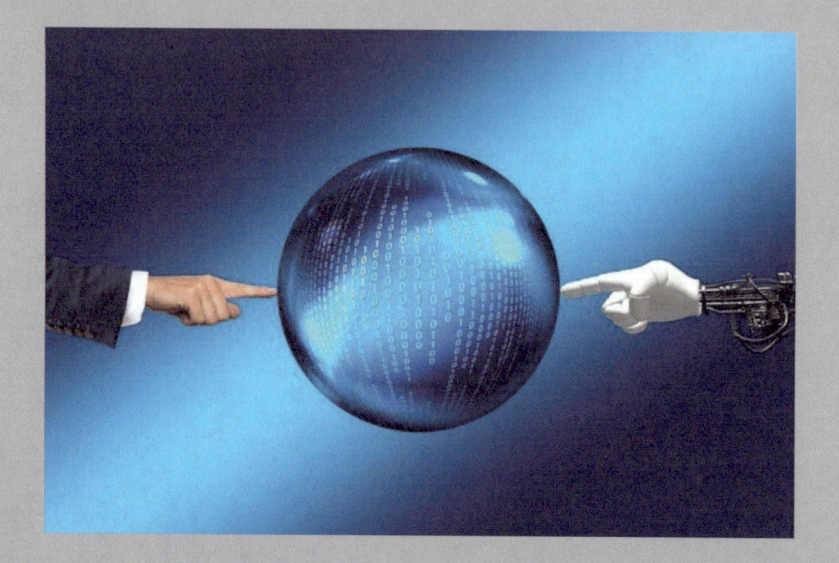

Artificial Intelligence in Corporate Communication

In conclusion, "Artificial Intelligence in Corporate Communication: Redefining the Game" has shed light on the transformative impact of AI on corporate communication strategies. It has provided insights into the opportunities and challenges that arise with the integration of AI and emphasized the importance of ethical considerations. As we embark on this AI revolution, let us embrace the possibilities, adapt to the changing landscape, and redefine the game of corporate communication through the power of AI.

About the Author

Bonnie Kurowski is a Industrial/ Organizational Psychologist. She has spent 18 years in Project Management, Change Management, and Learning and Development. As a Certified SCRUM Master, Coach, Trainer, ADKAR CM, LEAN Black Belt, and Sr. Instructional Designer, she entered the world of AI. She is currently a Transitional Consultant, assisting companies in the AI transition.

For more information, visit BonnieKurowski.com.

Made in the USA
Columbia, SC
27 February 2024